Warning!

Revelation is about to be fulfilled

Larry Wilson

Copyright © 1994

Wake Up America Seminars, Inc.

P.O. Box 273, Bellbrook, Ohio 45305

(513) 848-3322

P.O. Box 5003, Georgetown, Texas 78627

(512) 863-9009

First printing, March 1988
Second printing, June 1990
Third printing, January 1991
Fourth printing, November 1992
Fifth printing, June 1994

Published by

TEACH Services, Inc.

Route 1, Box 182

Brushton, New York 12916

Acknowledgements

This book is dedicated to those who *need* the return of our Saviour, our Lord and our Friend, Jesus.

This printing of 250,000 copies of the *Warning!* book has been made possible through the generosity of donors who wish to remain anonymous. Even though tens of thousands of readers will never know the identity of their benefactors — God knows what has been done in secret, and He will reward accordingly.

Special appreciation is also due Marty, Suzy and Shelley for their help on this edition. Even more, I am forever indebted to a dedicated staff (both paid and unpaid), generous volunteers and a rapidly growing number of wonderful people world-wide who understand this message and faithfully support this unique ministry.

Wake Up America Seminars, Inc. is a non-profit, educational organization. WUAS is not affiliated, endorsed nor sponsored by any religious organization. Our mission is to herald the salvation and imminent return of our Lord Jesus Christ through whatever means possible.

Warning! Revelation is about to be fulfilled

Table of Contents

Chapter 1

The rendezvous

This book was written for a simple reason: People need to know about coming events. I'm not referring to man-made events. I'm speaking of coming judgments from God. People need to know *what* God is about to do. They need to know *why* and they need to know *now*.

I believe the Bible predicts that God is going to send a devastating sequence of 14 events upon the earth. These coming events will not occur in random order, for Revelation clearly reveals their order. After they begin, billions of people will recognize — sooner or later — that these events are not random convulsions of nature. The cataclysmic events that will ignite the Great Tribulation will be recognized as Acts of God because people will see that these events and the reactions of earth's leaders have been foretold in the Bible. I believe the Great Tribulation will begin during 1994 or 1995 and terminate around 1998 with the second coming of Jesus.

The Bible indicates that God will accomplish a number of important matters during the Great Tribulation. First, He will awaken every person on earth to the fact that Jesus, the Judge of all mankind, is about to appear and require an account of each person's behavior. Second, God is about to expose the properties of sin to the human race because sin has a powerful effect that few recognize or understand. Third, God is going to expose the contents of every human heart by placing a comprehensive test of faith before all of us. Finally, the blasphemous claims of the world's religious systems will be silenced by God. He will demonstrate that salvation cannot be obtained through membership in *any* religious system. God is about to inform the world that salvation only comes through total commitment and submission to Jesus Christ.

I find that most of the prophetic interpretations we hear on radio and TV are misleading. Do not misunderstand. People can believe anything they choose to believe about the future, but what effect does belief or denial have on coming events? Almost everyone in Noah's day refused to believe a flood was coming. What effect did their denial have on the promised event? My point is that millions of people have been led to anticipate things that will never happen, and when the predicted events of Revelation begin, everything that can be shaken will be shaken. On that day many people will abandon their faith in God because their ministers misled them; even worse, pastors did not spiritually prepare their flocks for the trying circumstances their sheep will face. What is more bitter than the experience of misplaced trust? I mention this matter because most ministers, the *trusted* shepherds of the flock, either do not know about the coming events or they deny the seriousness of the 14 events that are just before us.

So, a very serious problem exists. What many people have been *led* to believe about God is not true. In the coming hour of tribulation, many unprepared Christians will become bitter. In their anger, frustration and fear, many people will hate God. Of course, such hatred will be misdirected. Here's a good question: Since most Christians have a Bible, who should God hold responsible for having faulty knowledge?

So, who is right?

It may sound as though I have no respect for long-established and well-respected experts on prophecy. Although my assertions may be bold, they are not directed at any individual or denomination. Nevertheless, it is my conviction that most prophetic teaching is wrong and misleading. I am often scolded for presenting prophetic ideas "that do not respect long established concepts of interpretation." In fact, about six years ago, a preacher scolded me saying, "And who do you think you are? Do you think that God would leapfrog His established agencies of higher learning and dedicated Christian scholars to give *you* special prophetic understanding?"

In the fields of physics, medicine, electronics, engineering and chemistry, it is highly unlikely that an ordinary person can make a significant discovery. However, in the case of prophetic discovery, the educational qualifications of the discoverer are not nearly as important as living at the right time, and through the guidance of the Holy Spirit, looking in the right places. The Holy Spirit can reveal more in 10 minutes than a person can learn on his own in 10 years. We live near the end of the world, and this is an asset that prophetic students in years past did not have. Today, we have access to a wealth of resources and information not previously available. We stand on higher ground. Our view of the past and the on-coming future is clearer because it is now possible to determine our chronological position within apocalyptic prophecy. In addition to this, history confirms a profound point about prophetic study: *Prophetic things are only understood on or about the time of fulfillment.* This principle is true because God only reveals what He wants people to know *when the time* for understanding arrives. So, if anything contributes to our study of prophecy in the 1990's it is this: The end of all things is at hand; therefore, everyone should be able to understand the coming fulfillment of the remaining prophecies for themselves.

Even though I say that most of the prophetic conclusions we hear today are wrong, I sincerely respect most expositors as dedicated Christian people. But when it comes to predicting the future, what gives one man an advantage over another? Do advanced degrees make predictions about the future more correct? No. In fact, it is almost impossible to find two highly educated Bible scholars who agree on Bible prophecy. So, how can ordinary people know which interpretations are true and which are false?

The ultimate test

No prophetic expositor can prove his predictions about the future. It is impossible to prove something that has not happened. The only way that any prediction can be deemed accurate is to clearly write it down before it comes to pass. Then, when the predicted event occurs, ordinary people can see the accuracy of the prediction. This simple procedure allows an impartial jury of observers to decide which predictions and interpretations are accurate by simply noting the presence or absence of the things predicted.

My predictions about coming events are quite different than all the others I have heard. I never intended to be different. I never intended to be a prophetic expositor. But, on the way to understanding the prophecies in

Daniel and Revelation for myself, I made a simple but profound discovery and this discovery has changed my life.

I have observed that there are 18 prophecies in the books of Daniel and Revelation *and each prophecy behaves in a consistent manner.* The events in each prophecy are in chronological order and they link together forming a very solid matrix! The key to understanding the 18 mysterious messages of Daniel and Revelation came when I discovered how each story chronologically links to the other 17 stories. Because of this simple discovery, I believe I have stumbled, by the grace of God and the ministry of the Holy Spirit, across a comprehensive and harmonious explanation of the elements in Daniel and Revelation.

If you disagree

If you disagree with my views on the future, do not waste time denigrating me. You cannot prove me wrong and I cannot prove myself right. Instead, put your convictions to the acid test as I have done. Write down the specifics of your conclusions about end-time events and publish them. Since neither of us can prove what the future holds, we must wait for the passage of time to reveal the accuracy of each person's view. In my case, the wait will not be long because time will soon expose whether my 1994-1998 time frame is right or wrong. If my conclusions prove to be faulty, I will publicly admit my mistakes and make the necessary adjustments in my thinking. If, however, the message in this book helps you find salvation through faith in Jesus Christ, that shall be reward enough for the 23 years of study I have devoted to Bible prophecy.

A prophetic peek

I believe the earthquake described in Revelation 8:5 could happen sometime during 1994. I may be off on the timing, but the year 1994 or 1995 appears to be significant. (See appendix.) I believe the earthquake will shake enough of our planet to be classified as a global event. Shortly after the earthquake, earth will experience a great meteoric storm of burning hailstones which will destroy billions (that's billions) of acres of rain forests, food crops and vegetation. In addition, billions of people (that's billions) around the world will be left homeless as a result of these unquenchable fires. These two calamitous events will be followed by other events of even greater consequence. Earth will experience two horrific asteroid impacts — the first will hit an ocean; the second will impact a continent. As I understand the prophecies, these and other Acts of God are central to the story contained in the book of Revelation. The fourth event will be a series of volcanic eruptions that will darken the sky for a long time. The absence of sunlight means there will be fewer crops. But, the fifth event will be in a class all by itself! The devil himself is going to appear on earth and claim to be Almighty God who has come to rescue the world. Because of his splendor and the marvelous miracles he will perform — even calling fire down from heaven — billions (that's billions) of people will receive him as God and obey him with a devotion that should only be reserved for Almighty God.

A calamity howler

Because I have understood for some time that the calamitous events predicted in Revelation would begin this decade, I wrote the first edition of this book in 1987 to warn people of the imminent fulfillment of Revelation. Even though this is now June, 1994 (and the fifth edition of this book), a few remaining months is not much time to distribute this unusual message very widely — especially since I am an obscure author and book distributors repeatedly turn me down. Additionally, most Christians are either confident with what their church leaders say about the future, or they are so consumed with the demands of life that they cannot dedicate significant time to personal Bible study.

Being a calamity howler is not a good job to have. Do not misunderstand. Those who know me personally know that I am a very positive person. By nature, I'm quick to laugh, and finding the funny side of life comes easy. I am not pessimistic nor am I negative about the end of the world. Instead, I am positive that the end is coming soon and we shall see Jesus in all His glory. I fear the sequence of events is so different than what most people expect that billions of people will be unprepared for the things that will occur before the second coming of Jesus.

This fifth edition has been reduced a few pages, but the message has not been diluted. Rather, it has been concentrated to give you a quicker understanding of the big picture. My goal is not to convince you, but to introduce you to a story that is about to begin — a story that will affect you and me. If, in the coming tribulation, we can understand God's purposes, hope will surface and sustain us through earth's darkest hour. Remember, no matter how dark the night or how extreme our needs, God is always present. God understands our situation. He knows our fears. He will not forsake His children.

I am not a prophet or a seer. I have not had visions or supernatural encounters. I am an ordinary person who has searched the Scriptures to find understanding. I can truthfully say that I have found the Bible to be "a lamp unto my feet and a light unto my path." The Bible is a book without compare and it is my most valuable possession.

Listen to the Holy Spirit

I cannot say much about the processes of interpretation (hermeneutics) that support the conclusions set forth due to the brevity of this book. Instead, this book introduces people to the discoveries I have found in Daniel and Revelation. If, after reading this book, you want to obtain a deeper understanding of how these conclusions are reached, a list of study materials is provided on the back pages of this book.

So, if you read this book before the predicted events come to pass, and if the Holy Spirit impresses you that this message is valuable, then you have reason enough to share this book with others. If you do not find this message to be true or valuable, pitch this book into the trash. Do not displace the voice of the Holy Spirit with the opinions of employers, friends, experts or family members. Study this message for yourself and listen for God to speak to you. Then decide if this matter is important.

Understanding the design

Perhaps a brief review of the personal struggle I had with overcoming preconceived ideas will help you as you consider new ideas regarding apocalyptic prophecy. Twenty-three years ago, I approached the study of Daniel and Revelation much differently than I now do. I was eager and determined to quickly solve the mysteries found in these two books. With new-birth innocence, I soon fell into the common prophetic trap of justifying what I thought I understood, and diminishing the importance of things that I did not understand. As time passed, I came to see my folly. How can one declare something to be insignificant when he does not understand what it is? How can one claim to have solved the prophetic puzzle when he has not placed every element in its rightful place? (As I count them, there are about 200 prophetic elements.)

When I realized my dilemma, my unfounded confidence in what I thought was true was shattered — my eschatology turned out to be undone. In my defeat, I became willing to go to ground zero. I prayed, "Oh God, let the Bible speak and I will listen — not to justify my views, but to understand Your truth." My prayer has not changed, and I continue to ask for wisdom. In the years that have followed, I have been led in a direction that was entirely new to me. Eventually, I came to see that understanding the master design of apocalyptic prophecy must come before I could understand the true meaning of its parts.

Everything in the physical world is governed by laws of design. Laws control the movement of electrons, the effects of gravity, the orbits of planets, and the behavior of all chemical substances. So, I wondered if laws of design governed the prophecies of Daniel and Revelation in the same manner. To my amazement, I discovered that they do. In other words, when God gave the prophecies to Daniel and John long ago, He followed a specific design or set of rules. Once we understand His laws of design, we can correctly interpret Daniel and Revelation! I'm convinced that God sealed up the knowledge of these laws of design until the end of time (1994-1998) was near. In fact, the Bible says the book of Daniel was sealed up until *the time of the end.* (Daniel 12:4,9) These two verses fully confirm this point: The *only* generation to correctly understand the prophecies of Daniel will be the *last* generation. Because the prophecies of Revelation follow the same laws of design as the prophecies of Daniel, the unsealing of Daniel produces the true meaning of Revelation. Remember, the truth about Daniel and Revelation can only be understood at the time of the end.

Since this is a small book, I will get right to the point. I have found four laws of design that consistently operate on the prophecies in Daniel and

Revelation. Please understand, I did not make up these four laws — no more than Sir Isaac Newton made up the law of gravity. Rather, I have observed four consistent behaviors in the 18 prophecies of Daniel and Revelation. Since I find these behaviors are always true, they must be laws of design. Here are the four laws in my words:

Rules for apocalyptic interpretation

1. Apocalyptic prophecy is defined as prophecy that covers a span of time. Each apocalyptic prophecy has a beginning and ending point in time, and the elements within each apocalyptic prophecy occur in the order in which they are given.
2. A fulfillment of apocalyptic prophecy occurs when all the specifications within the propnecy are met. This includes the chronological order of elements within the prophecy.
3. If an element is symbolic, the Bible will clearly identify the meaning of the symbol with relevant scripture.
4. The operation of the Jubilee calendar explains when time-periods are to be interpreted as a day for a year or when time is to be reckoned as literal.

I share these findings with you because the conclusions presented in this book are very different than the popular ideas being widely spread on prophecy today. The concept of interpreting prophecy according to the laws of design is a crucial matter to me because if there are no laws of design, then diversity of interpretation can be the only result. One person may say prophecy means one thing while another may say it means something else. Without rules or knowledge of the master design, how can an ordinary person know what is true and what is false?

If there is one correct meaning of prophecy, then religious affiliation should not matter. Whether one is Catholic, Protestant, Jew or Atheist, the truth about coming events will be seen by all. The Bible means what it says, and says what it means. Apocalyptic prophecy was given to man on the basis of what will happen instead of what might have been. So, in the final analysis, prophetic truth is not, nor has it ever been, dependent on the approval or even the understanding of man.

If the process of interpretation is harmonious with the laws of design that God used when constructing the prophecies, nothing can prevent us from reaching a correct understanding *before* the predicted events occur. I disdain the idea that a person can interpret the Bible by reading the headlines of a newspaper. Instead, we should be able to read the Bible and anticipate events that will be reported in newspapers later.

The net effect is this. If my understanding of the four laws of design is correct, then other people, following or observing the same laws, should be able to reach the same conclusions that I have without discussing the prophecies with me. Indeed, this has been the case. I have met a few people from various denominations who have come to similar conclusions. This has been most encouraging because truth is not private or parochial; that is, truth is true everywhere. Truth is universal.

When prophetic expositors fail to understand the laws of design, they have no choice but to realign newspaper reports with Bible texts to show some relevancy (or accuracy) for their prophetic claims. This is interpretation by hindsight — "Monday morning quarterbacking." So, the heart of prophetic study boils down to this: Without rules of interpretation, the need for adjustment and validity never ends. Political events can change quickly and those who base their prophetic understanding on newspaper headlines must continually adjust their claims. Because this is the prevailing method of interpretation, it has become impossible for laymen to nail down a simple, straight-forward explanation of what the Bible actually says about the future. Therefore, valid rules of interpretation are essential. Without them, the meaning of prophecy is nothing more than a guessing game.

Again, I must emphasize that my prophetic beliefs have nothing to do with future events. Believing that something will happen or denying that something will happen has no effect whatsoever on what will be. How many in Noah's day denied the flood was coming and what effect did their denial have on the promised event?

Prerequisites

To appreciate the prophetic conclusions produced by the laws of design, a person needs to correctly understand five basic doctrines. So far, I have not found a religious body which *fully* embraces all that these five doctrines offer, especially as they relate to the fulfillment of prophecy.

I realize that my assertion can sound arrogant, but this is not my attitude. I am simply saying that truth is larger than any denomination. Truth is not static. On the other hand, denominations are static. Denominations form when a body of people become *fixed* on ideas about truth. This is a perpetual dilemma for denominations because truth does not stand still as denominations do. God continues to unfold more truth. Knowledge continues to advance in medicine, physics, astronomy and in theology as well.

Because truth is ever advancing, those who stand still are left behind. For example, manufacturers constantly update their products as knowledge increases. The little computer on my desk today is more powerful than the world's largest computer 30 years ago. When knowledge increases, changes should occur. But, as religious bodies increase in size, they become more defensive about their beliefs or traditions. Many Christians will not investigate new ideas on prophecy because they fear deception. These people have been deceived already. They have been led to believe that they already know the truth, but God's truth is ever advancing. Which is worse — to believe that you already know the truth, or to refuse to examine a message that may have more truth? I find either position deadly.

Fortunately, God knows human beings. He knows our foolish ways. He also knows that He has been silent a long time. Soon He is going to expose all doctrines and prophetic conclusions for what they are. The fullness of truth will be seen clearly — and so will the great expanse of error. The catalyst, the coming Great Tribulation, will reveal what is true and what is not. God has ordained that the final events of earth will occur in such a manner that all religious doctrines will be tested and exposed for what they really are. This means that every religious body, church and person on earth will be shaken with the realization that truth has advanced and the need for updating has come. Who will be able to tolerate such a dramatic update in his religious thinking? Only those who *love truth* can adapt to the ever increasing revelation of truth. This is the central issue in Revelation's story. In the end-time, those who truly love God will clearly see Him and understand His truth. The Bible predicts this. (John 16:13, Revelation 22:6)

I believe Revelation's story indicates that before the tribulation is over, everyone will have to leave his or her denomination to join either God's people or the one-world government that will be established when the mark of the beast is implemented. I will say more about this later, but the point is that there will be a mass reduction in the number of religious affiliations before the tribulation is over. Our choices will be reduced to two.

Also, remember this point: No one can *prove* what the future holds. Man cannot prove something that has not happened. But, lack of proof does not lessen our need for understanding; rather, it increases our need for grasping the purposes and plans of God. So, every person must seek truth. It is a God-given joy and responsibility, and prophetic truth is confirmed by the harmony that comes from the sum of all prophetic parts. If we carefully follow the laws of design, our prophetic faith will be as secure as God allows.

Five doctrines

Here are five doctrines that we need to understand in order to fully appreciate the contents of apocalyptic prophecy:

1. The worship of God — His sovereign authority
2. The salvation of God — Our faith in His actions tested
3. The sanctuary of God — His process to save to man
4. The coming of God — His indignation with sin
5. The soul of man — Our eternal state

These expansive subjects cannot be presented in this small book even though they need to be addressed. For this reason, the reader is encouraged to obtain a copy of my book, *The Revelation of Jesus* which is described on the last page of this book.

A testing time

Bible prophecy not only explains how the end of the world will occur, but it also tells why it must occur. Since most prophetic expositors do not anticipate God's dramatic intervention in the affairs of man, they do not understand the coming drama. In addition, most Christians do not anticipate the test of faith that each of us must face. In fact, I have a number of friends who believe in a pre-tribulation rapture. They believe that the people of God are going to escape the coming tribulation. If they are correct, then Christians have nothing to worry about. But, if the rapture idea is false, then Christians need some rapture insurance. I believe we need a comprehensive understanding of God's plans and purposes because I have not been able to find a pre-tribulation rapture in the apocalyptic sequence of events given in Daniel and Revelation. Instead, I find that the dragon (the devil) and his global organization Babylon, is going to make war on the *last* generation of saints. (See Revelation 12:17; 13:7.)

So, I ask those who sincerely believe in a pre-tribulation rapture to consider the message in this book anyway — not for the purpose of changing your mind, but for the purpose of becoming acquainted with the events of the coming tribulation. If the passage of time proves that I am wrong about these things, I will be left with one consolation: I would have studied and worked just as hard if I had known the truth.

Futurism and historicism

There are several schools of thought on Bible prophecy and naturally, the two most popular views are diametrically opposed. They are very well defined and enthusiastically defended by scholars on both sides. The school of thought having the most followers is called futurism, and its origin can be traced back to the late 1500's. The two most prominent teachings of futurism are variations on the rapture and the restoration of the state of Israel. Even though futurism generates a lot of excitement and discussion, its significance will disappear the day God sends a global earthquake and meteoric showers of burning hail.

I believe futurism misses the mark in several areas, but especially in two important ones. First, as mentioned above, I find no support for a pre-trib or mid-trib rapture. Yes, I have read all the texts that are used to support the claim of a pre/mid-trib rapture. But, the *context* does not support the claim — especially within the sequence of apocalyptic prophecy. Consequently, I expect that many fine people will be overwhelmed when the Great Tribulation begins and they discover they are still on earth. Many will bitterly lament their unprepared state because they were erroneously led to believe that they would escape the tribulation. I'm afraid that millions will abandon their faith in God because they will be overwhelmed and disappointed with their church, their leaders, and their prophetic faith. This, of course, will make the devil very happy. When God's judgments begin, they will not know what or whom to believe.

Second, futurism does not recognize the supreme deception of all ages that is about to take place. The Bible states that the devil *himself* will occupy a physical body and appear at various places around the earth. In other words, futurists do not anticipate the brilliant and glorious appearing of the devil. Satan, in the radiant form of a god-man, will work mighty miracles. He will even call fire down out of heaven in full view of enormous crowds. Most of the world will believe he is Almighty God when, in reality, he is nothing less than that ancient serpent, the predicted Antichrist. This is a very serious flaw with futurism.

The older and less accepted school of thought is called historicism. The main doctrine of this school is that the papacy is the great Antichrist power of Daniel and Revelation. This doctrine developed in England during the 1300's when the venerable John Wycliff began to call for reformation within the Roman Church. His clarion call for the exaltation of Bible truth and the elimination of man-made doctrines angered prelates and popes for years. Wycliff did not know that his call for fidelity to Bible truth would culminate with the Protestant Reformation in the 18th century. The problem with historicism today is that it is still bashing the pope and the Roman Catholic Church as though the 18th century reformation was still going on.

Historicists fail to recognize that the world is also made up of other religious systems comprising billions of people. Admittedly, no religious system on earth today is equal with the Roman Catholic Church in political influence; however, there are other religious systems that deviate from Bible truth just as much as papal doctrine. Two religious systems have even a larger number of devoted subjects!

I find fault with the historical view of Revelation for two reasons: First, historicism teaches that the bulk of Revelation has been fulfilled. Consequently, disciples of this doctrine do not anticipate the soon fulfillment of Revelation. Since they believe that Revelation, for the most part, has been fulfilled, historicists will experience the same shock that futurists will experience when Revelation turns out quite differently than expected!

The second problem with the historical position is historicists teach that the seven-headed, ten-horned beast of Revelation 13 is the Roman Catholic Church, and its partner, the lamb-like beast, is the United States of America. These two powers, they believe, will rule over all the inhabitants of the earth and set up the mark of the beast. Yes, the papacy and the United States will be major players during end-time events, but they will not be the only players! This world is made up of many political and religious systems, and Revelation's story not only identifies many of them, it includes them all.

Opposite views produce the same effect

Both futurism and historicism, even though diametrically opposed to each other, produce the same erroneous conclusion. Futurists plan to be in Heaven while Revelation is being fulfilled, and historicists are convinced that most of Revelation has already happened! The bottom line from both schools is that an understanding of Revelation is not *essential* right now!

Faith and foolishness

Most people of Noah's day thought he was crazy for building a gigantic boat. That folly was only exceeded by his talk about a great flood of water. If you consider the days before the flood, Noah appeared to be very foolish — even insane. It is interesting to note that *none* of the scholars, scientists, engineers or popular evangelists went into the ark with Noah and his family! Why didn't the experts enter the ark? The Bible says, **"By faith Noah, when warned about things not yet seen, in holy fear built an ark to save his family. By his faith he condemned the world and became heir of the righteousness that comes by faith."** (Hebrews 11:7)

Noah built the ark on the basis of prophetic faith. That is why the experts did not get on the ark. Experts do not place much faith in God; they prefer the facts. The experts found no reason to believe Noah or God's warning delivered through Noah. The experts trusted in their own wisdom and lost everything. Noah, however, trusted in God and saved himself and his family.

God's silence

God *appears* to be silent because He has not openly interfered with the actions of man for many centuries. However, God is going to break His long-standing silence with our planet by sending His judgments. These judgments will come from the heavens as well as from deep within the earth. When they begin, sinners will know that "The Great Day of the Lord" has come. At that time everyone will experience the fear of Almighty God. I know this sounds like a fairy tale, but 30-60 days after the manifestations of God's wrath begins, I expect to see the formation of a religious union that reaches around the world. In addition to this, martial laws will be implemented in all nations almost immediately. When that day arrives, the leaders of earth will unwittingly begin to fulfill verses of Daniel and Revelation written more than two thousand years ago.

I am excited about the nearness of these events because I see that the stage is *now* set. The end-time players are in place. World leaders are ostensibly seeking for peace and unity — a one-world coalition of nations governed by international law. Global leaders say they want peace and safety for all peoples, but progress is slow. The basic problem is this: The heart of man is selfish. Greed, arrogance and pride are the root of madness, war and unrest. But, the coming judgments of God will change the political structures of the world overnight. God is about to grant control of the world to seven religious systems and ten political leaders. They don't know it yet, but this has been planned by God for thousands of years.

God largely misunderstood today

The character of God is poorly understood — even in America. Most men and women diminish His authority, glory and power, because He has not openly revealed Himself in the affairs of man in recent times. Isaiah though, was awed at God's great powers. Isaiah was also amazed at God's reluctance to show Himself as the Almighty. Isaiah wrote, **"Truly you are a God who hides himself, O God and Savior of Israel."** (Isaiah 45:15)

God's *apparent* silence comes as a consequence of sin. Just as offenses physically separate friends or family members, the offensiveness of sin has separated us from God's physical presence. As generations come and go, the knowledge of God dims. The reality of God becomes faint, and the longer we go without renewed evidence of God's authority and glory, the more silent He appears to be. In the vacuum of this silence, sin becomes more attractive and less offensive. Sinners become bold and defiant in transgression. Sin metastasizes. Violence, sorrow and suffering spring up like dandelions after a spring rain. Every night, the evening news confirms our slide toward depravity. Degenerate, even hideous sins are either justified or ignored. Sin has a strange effect on human beings — it causes sinners to minimize the effects or the guilt of their wrong doing. Think about this for a full two seconds: Sin causes human beings to deny their wrong doing! (How many in prison falsely maintain their innocence?)

The Bible reveals that God breaks His silence from time to time. He uses four judgments to limit the growth of sin. (Ezekiel 14:21) His four judgments are sword, famine, plague and wild beasts. In His infinite wisdom, God allows nations to rule until they fill up their cup of iniquity, and when they do, the Bible says that He removes them from power. (See Daniel 2:21; 4:16, Leviticus 18:24-27.) What makes this process so remarkable to me is that God, even within the chaos of sin, completely accomplishes His plans and purposes on this earth! We may try to explain the outcome of earthly events by analyzing the actions of the players, but this is only a limited view. Do not be naive and think that things happen by the prowess of man. Nothing happens in the universe without God's knowledge and permission. Even though we are not able to see God on His throne, we can know that He reigns over the kingdoms of man. God is sovereign. We may not see all that He is doing, but the evidence is right before our eyes. The Bible is clear — God is in control. How He maintains control is a mystery. That He does it without showing Himself is His silence.

God's silence is not too hard to penetrate if you really want to see and hear Him. The evidences of His handiwork are all around us if we want to acknowledge Him. However, if we do not want to give Him due respect, we can easily ignore Him and deny Him the recognition He is due. Thus, His silence complements our power of choice. God can either be the greatest and most wonderful being in the universe or, if we so choose, we can deny His existence. What a God! Perhaps the least understood element within God's character is His reluctance to awe His creatures with His powers and presence. His silence will be a topic of eternal discovery!

Very important point

When God breaks His silence by raining down His judgments upon earth, the events will be understood even though God will be grossly misunderstood. To appease God and stay His awful judgments, the world's religious and political systems will enact laws "honoring God" that will be contrary to what He actually wants! What God seeks from man is a repentant heart and a willing attitude. He calls men and women to live a life free of the damning power of sin. Even more, He grants men and women who put their faith in Him the power necessary for victory over sin. However, Revelation predicts that men and women will largely reject God's gracious offer of power over sin and resulting salvation. The hearts of many people have become hardened in rebellion because of love for sin. But this is not the end of the story. Revelation also predicts that the wicked will be marked by a spirit of intolerance when confronted with the Holy Spirit authority of God's messengers. A day is soon coming when evil men will punish and torture those who obey the living God of Heaven. The persecutors will think, like Pilate, that they can wash their hands of the guilt of these acts. But, God *never* ignores evil even though He may allow it to flourish for a season. God will avenge every evil deed and will see to it that each person receives double the pain in return for the pain they inflicted. (See Revelation 18:6 and Obadiah 1:15.)

In the context of His coming judgments, God's character and His behavior will be misrepresented and misinterpreted. This is the heart of Revelation's story. It is a story of a loving God visiting a planet in trouble. It is also a story about rebellious people and a world gone astray. Most people, when put to the coming test, will openly and conscientiously reject the clearest evidences of God's truth. They will unite themselves in rebellion against the Ten Commandments of the Most High God by obeying the laws of the coming glorious god-man, the Antichrist — the devil himself. God is going to allow Satan to physically appear all over the world because **"they refused to love the truth and so be saved."** (2 Thessalonians 2:10) Jesus said, "This is the verdict: Light has come into the world, but men loved darkness instead of light because their deeds were evil. Everyone who does evil hates the light, and will not come into the light for fear that his deeds will be exposed." (John 3:19-20)

So, as you read this book, keep in mind that the Bible underscores a glorious but sublime truth. God does not condemn a person for believing a lie. Rather, He only condemns those who willfully refuse to believe the truth! Think of it this way. If God places the clearest evidences of truth before His creatures and they refuse to agree with His principles of righteousness, what more can be done? Is life — whose source is God — a privilege or a right? Are rebellious creatures just as deserving of eternal life as submissive creatures? Where in this universe can a rebellious creature live in peace if God is omnipresent throughout His realm? These are thoughtful questions that we must address. The eternal kingdom of Heaven has a set of issues and considerations that go far beyond our brief life span of 70 years and the limits of travel we have today.

It is time to end this lengthy but essential introduction and step up to the microphone and deliver the message. If my conclusions are right, we are about to see the day when God breaks His silence. On that dreadful day, everyone will know that God's patience with sin and sinners has reached its limit. On that day, mortals on a tiny speck of a planet called Earth will know that Almighty God, Owner of the Universe, has summoned man to appear before His everlasting throne of righteousness.

Larry Wilson
June 1994

Chapter 2

The full cup principle

"I the Lord have spoken. The time has come for me to act. I will not hold back; I will not have pity, nor will I relent. You will be judged according to your conduct and your actions, declares the Sovereign Lord." (Ezekiel 24:14) A day is coming when God will break His silence with sin. It will happen suddenly and it will sever the past from the oncoming future. Life as we know it will immediately and irrevocably change. The world has yet to witness anything like the coming judgments of God, nor can it sustain more than one visitation. God will act suddenly and powerfully, and all the inhabitants of earth will be overwhelmed with His swiftness and intensity. In this context, the authority, character and actions of God will become a subject of profound interest and controversy.

So, what is Jesus about to do? The opening of the fourth seal explains, "When the Lamb opened the fourth seal... I looked, and there before me was a pale horse! Its rider was named Death, and Hades was following close behind him. They were given power over a fourth of the earth to kill by sword, famine and plague, and by the wild beasts of the earth." (Revelation 6:7,8) The opening of this seal marks the beginning of the time-period called, "The Great Tribulation." Because the coming calamity will be so extensive, God has promised that the tribulation will not exceed 1,335 days. (Daniel 12:12) During this time period of 3.6 years, 25% of Earth's 5.6 billion will perish. Such an assault on human beings can begin with nothing less than a direct order from Jesus, the Lamb that opens the fourth seal. So, why will the Lamb do this to us?

Isaiah explains, "See, the Lord is going to lay waste the earth and devastate it; he will ruin its face and scatter its inhabitants.... The earth will be completely laid waste and totally plundered. The Lord has spoken this word.... **The earth is defiled by its people; they have disobeyed the laws, violated the statutes and broken the everlasting covenant. Therefore a curse consumes the earth; its people must bear their guilt. Therefore earth's inhabitants are burned up, and very few are left."** (Isaiah 24:1-6)

Symbolic or literal — past or future?

Some people argue that the four judgments of the fourth seal are symbolic and therefore, not to be taken literally. Others say that the fourth seal happened long ago. Many argue that God does not kill people anyway. So what is the truth?

Let the Bible speak. Notice God's comments to Ezekiel (especially note the words that I have italicized): **"Son of man, if a country sins against** *me* **by being unfaithful and** *I* **stretch out my hand against it to cut off its food supply and send famine upon it and** *kill* **its men and their animals.... Or if** *I* **send wild beasts through that country and they leave it childless and it becomes desolate so that no one can pass through it because of the beasts.... Or if** *I* **bring a sword against that country and say, 'Let the sword pass throughout the land,' and** *I* *kill* **its men and their animals.... Or if** *I* **send a plague into that land and pour out my wrath upon it through bloodshed,** *killing* **its men and their animals.... For this is what the Sovereign Lord says: How much worse will it be when** *I* **send against Jerusalem** *my* **four dreadful judgments — sword and famine and wild beasts and plague — to** *kill* **its men and their animals.... They will come to you (Ezekiel), and when you see their conduct and their actions, you will be consoled regarding the disaster** *I* **have brought upon Jerusalem —** *every disaster I have brought upon it.* **You will be consoled when you see their conduct and their actions, for you will know that** *I have done nothing in it without cause,* **declares the Sovereign Lord."** (Ezekiel 14:13-23)

No one can intelligently say that God's four judgments of plague, famine, sword and wild beasts are symbolic after reading these verses. God's literal judgments kill literal people, and God personally claims responsibility the killing caused by these four judgments. God justified Himself to Ezekiel for doing such things by saying, **"I have done nothing in it without cause."** (Ezekiel 14:23) This matter calls for a close understanding of God's character. God has used sword, famine, plague and wild beasts in the past and He is going to use these four judgments again. They are specifically mentioned in the fourth seal.

The full cup principle

What causes God to send judgments upon human beings? Today, many people interpret God's silence or passiveness with evil to mean that He is either dead or indifferent to what we do. Others see His permissiveness as proof that He is disinterested in each person's day-to-day activities. For this reason, a growing number of people are committing horrible evil deeds, thinking that God does not see them nor will He hold each of them responsible for their actions. The truth is that we may not realize the strict accountability we must each give to God for every action! Solomon said, **"Now all has been heard; here is the conclusion of the matter: Fear God and keep his commandments, for this is the whole duty of man. For God will bring every deed into judgment, including every hidden thing, whether it is good or evil."** (Ecclesiastes 12:13,14)

Christians often talk and sing about God's mercy and His saving grace, but few openly talk about God's anger or wrath. Why? Are we afraid to know what makes God angry?

To put God's wrath into perspective, we need to review Bible history to observe that God follows a consistent principle in dealing with humanity. This principle is called the "full cup principle." The concept is so simple that a child can understand it. In essence, when a person, city, nation or body of people reach a certain level of decadence or wickedness, God's patience expires and He breaks His silence by using one or more of His divine judgments. If the situation is redeemable, His judgments are redemptive. If the situation is beyond redemption, His judgments are destructive.

Examples

The antediluvians filled up their cup: **"The Lord saw how great man's wickedness on the earth had become, and that every inclination of the thoughts of his heart was only evil all the time. The Lord was grieved** that he had made man on the earth, and his heart was filled with pain. So the Lord said, 'I will wipe mankind, whom I have created, from the face of the earth — men and animals, and creatures that move along the ground, and birds of the air — for I am grieved that I have made them.' " (Genesis 6:5-7) God destroyed the world with a flood in Noah's day because the antediluvians' cup of iniquity had reached full measure. God broke His silence by first warning the world through Noah what He was going to do, and then, He proceeded to destroy the inhabitants of the world as He promised. When divine love and mercy no longer produced repentance and reformation in the antediluvians, God's justice demanded destructive action.

The Amorites filled up their cup: **"Then the Lord said to him (Abraham), 'Know for certain that your descendants will be strangers in a country not their own, and they will be enslaved and mistreated four hundred years. But I will punish the nation they serve as slaves, and afterward they will come out with great possessions. You, however, will go to your fathers in peace and be buried at a good old age. In the fourth generation your descendants will come back here, for the sin of the Amorites has not yet reached its full measure.' "** (Genesis 15:13-16)

Did you notice the last sentence of the text above? God would give Canaan to Abraham's offspring only *after* the sins of the Amorites had reached full measure! Make no mistake about this. God does not take land from one nation to give to another. Canaan belonged to the Creator, and He would only give Canaan to Abraham's descendants *after* the Amorites had exhausted their chance of possessing that beautiful land. Keep in mind that ancient Israel's possession of Canaan was based on the *same* conditions applicable to the Amorites. Moses knew that possession of Canaan was conditional. So, he warned Israel: **"But be assured today that the Lord your God is the one who goes across ahead of you like a devouring fire. He will destroy them; he will subdue them before you. And you will drive them out and annihilate them quickly.... After the Lord your God has driven them out before you, do not say to yourself, 'The Lord has brought me here to take possession of this land because of my righteousness.' No, it is on account of the wickedness of these nations that the Lord is going to drive them out before you. It is not because of your righteousness or your integrity that you are going in to take** possession of their land; but on account of the wickedness of these nations...." (Deuteronomy 9:3-5) Here is an extremely important point: The Canaanites were driven out and/or destroyed when their cup of wickedness became full! When God's patience with the Canaanites reached its limit, He broke His silence by sending His wrath upon them! (Leviticus 18)

Ancient Israel and Babylon filled up their cups: At the time of the Babylonian captivity, God told Israel, **"But you did not listen to me... and you have provoked me with what your hands have made, and you have brought harm to yourselves.... Because you have not listened to my words, I will summon all the peoples of the north and my servant Nebuchadnezzar king of Babylon... and I will bring them against this land and its inhabitants and against all the surrounding nations. I will completely destroy them and make them an object of horror and scorn, and an everlasting ruin.... This whole country will become a desolate wasteland, and these nations will serve the king of Babylon seventy years. But when the seventy years are fulfilled, I will punish the king of Babylon and his nation, the land of the Babylonians, for their guilt... and will make it desolate forever."** (Jeremiah 25:7-12)

Notice this point: Israel was destroyed for provoking God, *and* so was Babylon! This is proof that God deals with the heathen just as He deals with those who know Him! In God's eyes, wickedness is wickedness. Each person, city, nation and kingdom has a cup and when it becomes full, God breaks His silence.

One more point about ancient Babylon must be made. When the mysterious handwriting appeared on the palace wall, Belshazzar, King of Babylon, suspected that God was sending the sword against him, so he summoned the prophet Daniel to interpret the handwriting. Before giving the interpretation, Daniel recounted the divine judgments the Most High had sent upon his arrogant grandfather, Nebuchadnezzar. Then Daniel said, **"But you his son, O Belshazzar, have not humbled yourself, though you knew all this. Instead, you have set yourself up against the Lord of heaven.... But you did not honor the God who holds in his hand your life and all your ways.... This is what these words mean: *Mene*: God has numbered the days of your reign and brought it to an end. *Tekel*: You have been weighed on the scales and found wanting. *Peres*: Your kingdom is divided and given to the Medes and Persians."** (Daniel 5:22-28)

New Testament examples

The full cup principle is also found in the New Testament. Paul warned the sexually immoral Romans, **"...you are storing up wrath against yourself for the day of God's wrath, when his righteous judgment will be revealed. God will give to each person according to what he has done. But for those who are self-seeking and who reject the truth and follow evil, there will be wrath and anger."** (Romans 2:5,6,8) Compare these verses with Paul's statement in 2 Corinthians 5:10: **"For we must all appear before the judgment seat of Christ, that each one may receive what is due him for the things done while in the body, whether good or bad."** Paul understood why the wrath of God was coming. He told the believers in Colosse, **"Put to death, therefore, whatever belongs to your earthly nature: sexual immorality, impurity, lust, evil desires and greed, which is idolatry. Because of these, the wrath of God is coming."** (Colossians 3:5,6)

Paul encouraged the believers in Thessalonica to be patient in their suffering until the enemies of Jesus had filled up their cup. **"...You suffered from your own countrymen the same things those churches (in Judea) suffered from the Jews, who killed the Lord Jesus and the prophets and also drove us out. They (the Jews) displease God and are hostile to all men in their effort to keep us from speaking to the Gentiles so that they may be saved. In this way they always heap up their sins to the limit. The wrath of God has come upon them at last."** (1 Thessalonians 2:14-16) When Paul wrote this epistle, he knew that the Jews had filled up their cup and that they were doomed to destruction by the Romans. The promised destruction occurred in A.D. 70. (Luke 21:22)

Jesus condemns Israel using full cup principle

Jesus explained the full cup principle in a discourse with the Pharisees. After pronouncing seven curses on the leaders of Israel for their religious bigotry and hypocrisy, Jesus said, **"Fill up, then, the measure of the sin of your forefathers! You snakes! You brood of vipers! How will you escape being condemned to hell?"** (Matthew 23:32,33) Again, the point is made. When a nation or individual reaches the limit of divine forbearance, God breaks His silence. His mercy with sin and sinners has a limit. Jesus concluded His denunciation of the Jews saying, **"O Jerusalem, Jerusalem, you who kill the prophets and stone those sent to you, how often I have longed to gather your children together, as a hen gathers her chicks under her wings, but you were not willing. Look, your house is left to you desolate."** (Matthew 23:37,38) Later, Jesus predicted the destruction of Jerusalem *as a fulfillment* of God's wrath: **"When you see Jerusalem being surrounded by armies, you will know that its desolation is near. Then let those who are in Judea flee to the mountains, let those in the city get out, and let those in the country not enter the city. For this is the time of punishment in fulfillment of all that has been written."** (Luke 21:20-22)

Does God kill people?

From time to time, scholars assert that God does not kill nor destroy people. They say, "God just steps aside and turns evil people over to the natural consequences of sin which brings death and destruction. In some cases," they claim, "God turns people over to the devil and the devil kills or destroys them."

The justification for this view of God is false. This position ignores the weight of evidence found throughout the entire Bible and exclusively focuses on two prominent aspects of God's character. In simple terms, advocates of this view say that God is love. Because He is love, He does not violate His character of love by doing evil (killing). (1 John 4:8) Second, they claim that God would not break His own law; namely, **"Thou shalt not kill."** (Exodus 20:13, KJV) These two points are thought to prove that God neither destroys nor kills. Rather, they claim, God simply steps out of the way when people become totally evil and He either allows sin to take its natural, destructive course or He turns them over to the devil — allowing Satan to do whatever he wishes.

Falsehoods about God's character do a lot of damage when they are partially true. (A good lie is 99% truth.) So, this falsehood — that God does not kill or destroy — has gained a footing with those who ignore the weight of evidence found throughout the Bible.

True, God is love and He has a wonderful purpose for His creatures. He loves man, He works with man, and He desires the best for man. However, He requires man to live within certain boundaries — physical and moral. For example, the law of momentum says that mass times velocity equals momentum. A 3,000 pound car doing 60 miles-per-hour has a lot of momentum. Suppose the driver gets drunk and his car hits a concrete object and the driver dies as a result. Did God kill the driver? No. The law of momentum did. So, there is validity to the claim that sin has its consequences. But the question remains, did a God of love create the law of momentum that killed the drunk driver? Yes, God created the law of momentum, and He desires us to respect His laws. But, if a person chooses to get drunk, and then violates the law of momentum, we would have to say that the drunk killed himself.

What about the sixth commandment, **"Thou shalt not kill?"** Would God violate His own commandment and kill people? The answer to this question is most important, so try to follow closely. The "murder commandment" is not exclusive. Within God's rules for life, there are a few occasions where death can be inflicted *without breaking* God's law. Notice what the Lord told Noah on his exit from the ark: **"And for your lifeblood I will surely demand an accounting. I will demand an accounting from every animal. And from each man, too, I will demand an accounting for the life of his fellow man. Whoever sheds the blood of man, by man shall his blood be shed; for in the image of God has God made man."** (Genesis 9:5,6) This verse shows that God commanded murderers be put to death by other men. Capital punishment is not the invention of man. The Bible reveals that capital punishment comes from the mind of God — not man. (See also Leviticus 20.)

When the children of Israel were in the desert, God spoke the Ten Commandments to them. At that time, God also elaborated more fully on the terms and conditions for capital punishment. **"These are to be legal requirements for you throughout the generations to come, wherever you live. Anyone who kills a person is to be put to death as a murderer only on the testimony of witnesses. But no one is to be put to death on the testimony of only one witness. Do not accept a ransom for the life of a murderer, who deserves to die. He must surely be put to death."** (Numbers 35:29-31)

The point here is that God does not break His own law by requiring men to put murderers to death. A person has to incorporate *all* that God has said about killing to understand His *intent* for laws about life and death. So, the people who claim that God cannot kill because He does not break His own law do not understand the intent of the law of God — specifically, the Ten Commandments! When God said, **"Thou shalt not kill,"** He commanded that we are not to kill one another. However, if someone chooses to commit murder, God declares that the murderer must be put to death and the next of kin can kill the murderer *without incurring guilt.* Notice, **"[If] the avenger of blood finds him [the murderer] outside the city [of refuge], the avenger of blood may kill the accused without being guilty of murder."** (Numbers 35:27) If sinful man can kill without incurring guilt under certain circumstances, so can God.

Underlying principle

The underlying principle behind capital punishment is atonement. God requires atonement for sin. In God's order, there is no forgiveness for sin; rather, there is only atonement for sin. This is why Jesus died on the cross. He was slain for our sins. We may say that our sins are forgiven, but this is not the whole story. The sins of believers can be transferred to Jesus because He atoned for them by shedding His blood. He is our atonement. If the Old Testament sanctuary service teaches us anything, it is this: God requires atonement for all wrong doing. **"For the life of a creature is in the blood, and I have given it to you to make atonement for yourselves on the altar; it is the blood that makes atonement for one's life."** (Leviticus 17:11) **"In fact, the law requires that nearly everything be cleansed with blood, and without the shedding of blood there is no forgiveness."** (Hebrews 9:22)

Those individuals who claim that God does not kill or destroy people cannot explain the phenomenon of death on the firstborn of men and animals at the time of the Exodus. The Lord warned Moses that if blood was not found on the doorposts, *He* would slay the firstborn of each family, whether animal or man! **"On that same night *I* will pass through Egypt and strike down every firstborn—both men and animals—and *I* will bring**

judgment on all the gods of Egypt. *I am the LORD.*" (Exodus 12:12, italics mine)

This is an important point. If God does not kill, then who killed the eldest (the highest ranking) family member of men and animals in Egypt? If we say the devil did it, then we have to conclude that God and the devil were partners in the killing. But, we know that God does not *use* the devil to accomplish His works of righteousness. Furthermore, if God simply turned His back on the firstborn in Egypt and *allowed* the devil to kill this select group of people, then God would be an accomplice to murder. (God says that if one has the opportunity to prevent harm, and he does nothing about it, he becomes an accomplice to the harm committed and shares in its guilt. Ezekiel 3:17-21) But, the real point here is whether we can take God at His word. Does God claim that He kills people? Notice what the Lord told Moses: **"See now that I myself am He! There is no god besides me. I put to death and I bring to life, I have wounded and I will heal, and no one can deliver out of my hand."** (Deuteronomy 32:39)

The deaths of the firstborn in Egypt reveal something important about the character of God. He gave Pharaoh and his court nine plagues to convince them that He was Sovereign, but Pharaoh refused to recognize the manifestations of God's authority. During the Great Tribulation, history will be repeated. Men and women will refuse a direct order from the Almighty and they will receive His plagues! When men and women openly rebel against God, what more can He do? If we come to a place where we willfully refuse to recognize the difference between right and wrong, what are God's options? God killed the firstborn of Egypt as an object lesson for Israel and as punishment for Egypt. The punishment for Egypt was due to open rebellion against the authority of God. The object lesson for Israel was that someday, the Father would give human beings the power to kill His "firstborn" Son on Calvary so that atonement could be made for our sins. (John 19:10,11)

Incidently, three people were killed outright in the book of Acts under interesting circumstances. Read Acts 5:1-11 and Acts 12:23 and see if you can determine who did the killing. Also examine 2 Kings 1:1-17 and see who destroyed 102 men with fire. Read Isaiah 37:36 and see who killed 185,000 men. These texts should help to dismiss any doubt on this subject.

God's judgments and His covenant

Many, many instances of the full cup principle can be found in the Bible. However, the heart of this matter centers on the relationship that exists between man and God's everlasting covenant with mankind. To appreciate this statement, a few remarks are necessary.

Human beings are, for the most part, ignorant of all the forces that affect them. Again, consider the physical law of momentum. When you are riding in a car at 60 miles-per-hour (mph), you do not feel the powerful force called momentum. However, if your car crashed into the concrete support of an overpass at 60 mph, the law of momentum would require that certain reactions occur. The amount of energy released in a sudden stop like this is more than most people could survive.

In ancient times, the law of momentum was not significant because no one could reach the speed of 60 mph unless they fell off something quite high; however, the law of momentum existed then just as it does now. My point is that momentum was once unimportant, but now that we travel at 60+ mph, it is very important.

In a similar way, God's everlasting covenant with mankind has always existed. Even though billions of people have lived and died since the creation of the world, and most people were not aware of His covenant, it has always existed. This covenant, like the law of momentum, is universal and everlasting. The covenant may have been obscure in times past, but this obscurity will change dramatically when the judgments of God begin. God's everlasting covenant with human beings, in simple form, is like a Valentine greeting. It says: If you will be my people, I will be your God. (Ezekiel 37:26,27)

Paul understood the everlasting covenant. He says that non-Jews (Gentiles) belong to God if they live up to everything they know to be right. They may be ignorant of His covenant, but God accepts them anyway. Paul says, **"Indeed, when Gentiles, who do not have the law, do by nature things required by the law, they are a law for themselves, even though they do not have the law."** (See Romans 2:14; Acts 10:34,35.)

The point is that God always deals with mankind on the basis of His covenant. He consistently administers justice and mercy on the basis of universal law and not arbitrary whim. He is exceedingly patient, fair and forgiving and yet, there is a limit to divine kindness. The expulsion of Lucifer and one-third of Heaven's angels before the creation of the world proves that God's creatures can pass the point of divine forbearance. (Ezekiel 28:16,17) So historically, the Bible points out that God's redemptive judgments have fallen upon humanity when the limits of divine forbearance have been reached. The Bible also reveals that when His warning judgments fail to bring about repentance and reformation, God sends destructive judgments to terminate the rebellious party and check the growth of sin.

The covenant broken

God's four judgments — sword, famine, plague and wild beasts — are first mentioned as a group shortly after the Exodus. (Deuteronomy 32:24,25) When God called Israel out of Egypt, He clearly laid out the terms and conditions of His everlasting covenant to Israel. This covenant confuses a lot of people and consequently, their theology. Yet, the terms of this covenant are quite simple. In essence, God's everlasting covenant with mankind has always been: If you will be my people, I will be your God. This covenant is still intact today. (See Genesis 17:7; Exodus 6:7; Leviticus 26:11,12; Deuteronomy 7:6-8, 28:9 and Jeremiah 11:1-5.) It is extended to every man, woman and child. In fact, the good news of salvation — the gospel — is an explanation of the everlasting covenant. The invitation to accept this covenant and its terms will go rapidly throughout the world when the judgments of God begin. (Revelation 14:6,7) God's covenant invitation will reach every nation, language and living person within 1,260 days! (Revelation 11:3) The message will be delivered by God's 144,000 "hand-picked" messengers. (Revelation 7:3)

Needless confusion

Many Bible teachers are confused about God's covenant with ancient Israel and the everlasting covenant. This confusion stems from two faulty concepts. First, they think that God's covenant, given to Abraham and his descendants in Genesis 17, was exclusive to Abraham and his descendants. Second, they believe that God's covenant to Abraham and his biological descendants is irrevocable. When these two concepts are combined, it is easy to see why many people erroneously conclude that the nation of Israel today is an extension of God's promises to Abraham. This concept is contrary to the plainest Scriptures.

The New Testament clearly indicates that when Jesus died on Calvary, He opened the covenant to "whosoever will!" After Calvary, the promises offered by the covenant were no longer exclusive to the biological Jew. Paul said, **"There is neither Jew nor Greek [Gentile], slave nor free, male nor female, for you are all one in Christ Jesus. If you belong to Christ, then you are Abraham's seed, and heirs according to the [covenant] promise."** (Galatians 3:28-29)

Carefully notice what Paul told the Gentiles in Ephesus: **"Therefore, remember that formerly you who are Gentiles by birth and called 'uncircumcised' by those who call themselves 'the circumcision' (that done in the body by the hands of men)—remember that at that time you were separate from Christ, excluded from citizenship in Israel and foreigners to the covenants of the promise, without hope and without God in the world. But now in Christ Jesus you who once were far away have been brought near through the blood of Christ. For he himself is our peace, who has made the two one and has destroyed the barrier, the dividing wall of hostility, by abolishing in his flesh the law with its commandments and regulations. His purpose was to create in himself one new man out of the two, thus making peace, and in this one body to reconcile both of them to God through the cross, by which he put to death their hostility. He came and preached peace to you who were far away and peace to those who were near. For through him we both have access to the Father by one Spirit. Consequently, you are no longer foreigners and aliens, but fellow citizens with God's people and members of God's household."** (Ephesians 2:11-19) So, the point stands clear. Biological Jews are not exclusive owners or benefactors of the covenant. The covenant belongs to anyone, Jew or Gentile, willing to live by faith in Jesus. (John 3:16)

When God gave His covenant to Abraham, Abraham became a trustee of God's work on Earth. Many scholars refer to this covenant as the Abrahamic covenant. Yet, if you will read Genesis 17, you will find that God calls it *His* covenant nine times. The covenant between God and Abraham was not a covenant for the exclusive benefit of Abraham's descendants. Rather, God's everlasting covenant with mankind was placed in trust with Abraham. Abraham and his descendants were to be trustees of the everlasting covenant. During the time they met the terms of trusteeship, they would be especially blessed to carry the good news of salvation to the Gentiles. The everlasting covenant was not given to the Jews exclusively because God loves all the people in the whole wide *world!* (For God so loved the world....) Neither was the selection of Abraham's descendants as trustees irrevocable. (Romans 11:22-25) Unfortunately, the descendants of Abraham became spiritually arrogant. They thought they were the exclusive objects of God's affection, and time after time, this led to their downfall.

Israel lost their status as the chosen people of God at the end of the 70th week (Jubilee year, A.D. 33) because they violated the terms of trusteeship. New Testament theology is based on the fact that soon after the death of Christ (A.D. 30), the disciples recognized that Israel had lost its trusteeship of the gospel. (Matthew 23:38) The distinction between Jew and Gentile disappeared. Now, in Christ, there is neither male nor female. There is neither Jew nor Gentile, for the trustees of the covenant are those who follow Christ! (See Romans 11:17 and Galatians 3:28,29.)

Let us go back and prove that Israel's status as representatives of God was conditional. Moses summarized Israel's responsibility to God's covenant saying, **"Love the Lord your God with all your heart and with all your soul and with all your strength. If you fully obey the Lord your God and carefully follow all his commands I give you today, the Lord your God will set you high above all the nations on earth. All these blessings will come upon you and accompany you if you obey the Lord your God.... However, if you do not obey the Lord your God and do not carefully follow all his commands and decrees I am giving you today, all these curses will come upon you and overtake you.... The Lord will send on you curses, confusion and rebuke in everything you put your hand to, until you are destroyed and come to sudden ruin because of the evil you have done in forsaking him."** (Deuteronomy 6:5, 28:1-20)

The point we have to understand is that God's covenant with all of mankind is everlasting. But, the trusteeship — the privilege of delivering the gospel to others — is always conditional. (See Deuteronomy 28 and Ezekiel 18.)

The truth about the consequences

The Lord forewarned ancient Israel that if they ignored the terms of the trusteeship, there would be severe consequences. Why? Because His holy name would be profaned in the sight of nations. And what did Israel do? Israel profaned the name of God. **"Therefore say to the house of Israel, 'This is what the Sovereign Lord says: It is not for your sake, O house of Israel, that I am going to do these things, but for the sake of my holy name, which you have profaned among the nations where you have gone. I will show the holiness of my great name, which has been profaned among the nations, the name you have profaned among them. Then the nations will know that I am the Lord, declares the Sovereign Lord, when I show myself holy through you before their eyes.' "** (Ezekiel 36:22,23) (Also see Malachi 1:14, Leviticus 20:3, Jeremiah 34:16 and Ezekiel 20:9.) God is jealous for His name and no one can willfully dishonor Him and His covenant without consequence. (Even human beings have laws against libel and slander.)

We must also understand that God's covenant is not a covenant between equals. It is a covenant between Almighty God and mortal man — the Creator and the created. So, the everlasting covenant — first given to Adam, renewed to Noah and extended to Abraham and his descendants — not only contains a great privilege, it also contains a great responsibility!

The Bible makes it clear that this covenant is still intact today! The covenant is sometimes called the gospel. Notice what Paul says, **"For we also have had the gospel preached to us, just as they [ancient Israel] did; but the message they heard was of no value to them, because those who heard did not combine it with faith."** (Hebrews 4:2) The apostle John calls the gospel the *eternal* gospel and he saw it proclaimed to the *whole world* just before Jesus appears. He wrote, **"Then I saw another angel flying in midair, and he had the eternal gospel to proclaim to those who live on the earth—to every nation, tribe, language and people."** (Revelation 14:6) Look at this text and ask yourself this question: If there is an *eternal* gospel as Revelation 14:6 says, then the gospel that is proclaimed at the end-time had to exist before Adam, Noah and Abraham lived on the earth — didn't it?

In other words, the covenant (eternal gospel) passed down to Abraham is still valid today because Abraham is the father of *many* nations — not just Israel. (Genesis 17:4) This covenant, the gift of salvation, is available to every person through Christ. When God's judgments begin (the opening of the fourth seal), the eternal gospel explaining God's covenant will be completely revealed in all its beauty because the sincere in heart will want to know the will of the living God! This is why Jesus said, **"And this gospel of the kingdom will be preached in the whole world as a testimony to all nations, and then the end will come."** (Matthew 24:14)

God warns of His four judgments

Israel was warned about the consequences of violating God's covenant at the time of their exodus. God said, **"But if you will not listen to me and carry out all these commands... then I will do this to you: I will bring upon you sudden terror, wasting diseases and fever that will destroy your sight and drain away your life.... I will break down your stubborn pride and make the sky above you like iron and the ground beneath you like bronze. Your strength will be spent in vain, because your soil will not yield its crops.... I will send wild animals against you... destroy your cattle and make you so few in number that your roads will be deserted.... I will bring the sword upon you to avenge the breaking of the covenant.... I will send a plague among you.... I will lay waste the land.... I will scatter you among the nations...."** (Leviticus 26:14-33)

Look closely at the words in the text and see if you can find the four judgments. You will find famine, wild animals, sword and plague. These are specifically mentioned. In addition to the four judgments, notice that sudden terror is also mentioned. This is how God breaks His silence. He sends sudden terror upon nations when their cup of sin and rebellion becomes full. Paul tells us that this is what God is going to do in the last days. He says, **"While people are saying, 'Peace and safety,' destruction will come on them suddenly, as labor pains on a pregnant woman, and they will not escape."** (1 Thessalonians 5:3)

Bible history is clear

The Bible explains the way God implements His four judgments. Notice these instances:

Sword: God raises up military leaders to send the sword wherever He wants it. From Jeremiah 25:9 we learn that God sent His *servant,* King Nebuchadnezzar, against Jerusalem. Nebuchadnezzar did not know that he was a servant of the Most High God at the time! Nevertheless, God used the pagan king to destroy Jerusalem. In the same way, God overthrew the empire of Babylon through Darius, another unwitting servant of God. (Daniel 5:30,31) The Bible also says that King Cyrus was a servant of God. (See Ezra 1:1 and Isaiah 44:28, 25:1.) It is especially interesting to note that God is able to accomplish His plans without forcing His will on any individual! The point is that God raises up military leaders to take the sword wherever He wants, even though generals choose to do what they want to do.

Famine: God sends famine at times and in places to accomplish His purposes. In Genesis 41, God sent seven years of famine to Egypt, and in the process, removed Joseph from prison and put him on the throne. This amazing promotion for Joseph opened the way for the descendants of Abraham to move to Egypt! (Genesis 15:12-16)

In 2 Samuel 21:1, the Bible says, **"During the reign of David, there was a famine for three successive years; so David sought the face of the Lord. The Lord said, 'It is on account of Saul and his blood-stained house; it is because he put the Gibeonites to death.' "** Clearly, the three-year famine came as a direct result of Saul's disobedience.

In 2 Kings 8:1, we learn of a seven-year famine sent by the Lord: **"Now Elisha had said to the woman whose son he had restored to life, 'Go away with your family and stay for a while wherever you can, because the Lord has decreed a famine in the land that will last seven years.' "**

Perhaps one of the best known famines recorded in the Bible happened during the days of Elijah and King Ahab. Notice what James says: **"Elijah was a man just like us. He prayed earnestly that it would not rain, and it did not rain on the land for three and a half years. Again he prayed, and the heavens gave rain, and the earth produced its crops."** (James 5:17,18)

Plague: Plagues can come in numerous forms. We think of bubonic plague or cholera as a plague, but the word *plague* means anything troublesome or afflicting. God sent several plagues upon Pharaoh and Egypt to impress them that He wanted His people set free. These plagues included frogs, water-to-blood, gnats, flies, boils, hail, locusts, darkness, etc. (See Exodus 8-10.) The Lord killed 10 of the 12 spies with a plague for giving a bad report about the Promised Land! (Numbers 14:37) More than 14,700 people died of a plague in a wilderness rebellion started by Korah. (Numbers 16:49) On one occasion, God sent a plague that killed 24,000 people for sexual immorality! (Numbers 25:9) On another occasion, God sent a plague upon Israel and killed 70,000 people because King David disobeyed the Lord and took a census. (1 Chronicles 21:14-16) The point is that God sends plagues upon people to kill them if their evil ways warrant such action! Notice the threat that will be presented to the inhabitants of earth during the Great Tribulation: **"A third angel followed them and said in a loud voice: 'If anyone worships the beast and his image and receives his mark on the forehead or on the hand, he, too, will drink of the wine of God's fury, which has been poured full strength into the cup of his wrath. He will be tormented with burning sulfur in the presence of the holy angels and of the Lamb.' "** (Revelation 14:9-10)

Wild beasts: Wild beasts, like plagues, come in many forms. Peter described them saying, **"I looked into it (the sheet) and saw four-footed animals of the earth, wild beasts, reptiles, and birds of the air."** (Acts 11:6) The creatures of earth are wild beasts. So how does God use them? The Lord clearly warned Jeremiah how wild beasts would .be used to accomplish His deadly purpose upon Israel: **" 'I will send four kinds of destroyers against them (Israel),' declares the Lord, 'the sword to kill and the dogs to drag away and the birds of the air and the beasts of the earth to devour and destroy.' "** (Jeremiah 15:3) The Bible says that God sent poisonous vipers into the camp of Israel when they complained against Him. (See Numbers 21.) One family of "wild beasts" that may be influential in the future is insects. Killer bees, fleas, fire ants, swarms of locusts and other tiny creatures can cause unbelievable damage! Notice that God promised Israel that He would restrain the wild beasts if they would repent of their idolatry and love and obey Him. God said, **"I will make a covenant of peace with them (Israel) and rid the land of wild beasts so that they may live in the desert and sleep in the forests in safety."** (Ezekiel 34:25)

Back to the fourth seal

"When the Lamb opened the fourth seal, I heard the voice of the fourth living creature say, 'Come!' I looked, and there before me was a pale horse! Its rider was named Death, and Hades was following close behind him. They were given power over a fourth of the earth to kill by sword, famine and plague, and by the wild beasts of the earth." (Revelation 6:7,8)   There is evidence throughout the Bible that God has used His four judgments to deal with peoples and nations of the world when their cup of sin became full. The Bible also reveals that He only uses these judgments when sin and rebellion reach a point where His love and mercy have no redeeming effect. (See Ezekiel 5.) So, the judgments described in the fourth seal are literal and should be taken most seriously. As a matter of fact, if the population of planet Earth is 5.6 billion today, then 25% of that number would be 1.4 billion casualties!

A billion and a half casualties tells us that God is willing to sacrifice many for the salvation of others. After all, didn't He sacrifice His own Son for the salvation of all? We cannot conceptualize the breadth of God's interest in our salvation without considering the extensive destruction of the fourth seal. To some, this may sound terribly cruel and unfair. However, if the coming of Jesus is delayed another century, all 5.6 billion people currently living on earth would die anyway because the wages of sin is death. By accelerating the death of some people, others will be saved. This is a strange thing to say, but God is left — at times — with no other option but to destroy many to save a few. Remember the flood?

One last point. If we study the judgments which will come upon the Earth, we will get an appreciation for the dominion of God's law. Understand that God's wrath is not like our temper. His anger is justified. The coming 14 judgments have a purpose. The seven first plagues are for the saving of mankind. The seven last plagues are reserved for the destruction of those who chose to rebel against His authority. Keep in mind that God will fairly judge those who perish in His forthcoming judgments, just as He now judges all who die. God is more than fair.

How will the four judgments come?

Revelation's story explains how and when the four judgments of the fourth seal will be suddenly released. Without getting lost in all the prophetic parts, here is a brief explanation.

Ever since March 20, 1994 (see appendix), I believe that God has had four angels holding back the four winds of His judgments — sword, famine, plague and wild beasts. Winds symbolize destruction. Four winds symbolize global destruction. (See Genesis 41:27, Exodus 10:13, Job 1:19, Psalm 11:6, and Jeremiah 30:23.)   After God selects and empowers 144,000 people to proclaim the terms and conditions of the eternal gospel, the four angels will let the four winds of destruction go. (Revelation 7:1-4) The four winds are God's four judgments — sword, famine, plague and wild beasts — all identified in the fourth seal.

Then, 144,000 evangelists, strategically located in every country on Earth, will explain the purposes of God's judgments, and they will proclaim a comprehensive message about salvation which includes the imminent appearing of Jesus. The everlasting covenant and its terms of salvation will be revealed. The proclamation of the 144,000 will ignite religious persecution. Of course, truth infuriates those who love evil. The more powerful the truth, the greater the persecution. World leaders will do everything possible to appease an angry God. But, their efforts will be fruitless. What God wants of each person is a willful heart not legislated righteousness.

About two years (plus or minus) after the fourth seal judgments begin, the devil himself will appear and claim to be God in the flesh. To make his dominion of earth complete, the devil will demand that his followers kill the 144,000 and all who follow them. The net effect is that everyone on earth will be engulfed in the Great Tribulation. If you serve the true God, you will receive the wrath of the devil. If you join with the devil and the majority of the world, you will receive the wrath of God. Whose side will you join? Whose wrath will you choose to bear?

Seven trumpets

Here are some important things to watch for. The judgments described in the fourth seal will begin suddenly. (1 Thessalonians 5:3) I anticipate they will appear in 1994 or 1995. The four judgments of the fourth seal will come first in the form of seven trumpets. Later, they occur again in the form of seven last plagues. In other words, sword, famine, plague and wild beasts are found in the seven trumpets and in the seven last plagues. The time-period of the seven trumpets is redemptive while the time-period of the seven last plagues is destructive.

We must listen to the 144,000

The 144,000 of Revelation 7 are people in whom God grants special powers. (See Luke 9 for an example.) The 144,000 will be empowered by the Two Witnesses which are the Bible and the Holy Spirit. The 144,000 will be human agents through whom the Two Witnesses will reach every person. Like Moses and Elijah, the 144,000 will perform many miracles to convince people that their message is sent from God. They will explain what God is doing and why. Just as Pharaoh hardened his heart when Moses stood before him, many in our day will harden their hearts against God's messengers.

The Holy Spirit will stir every heart, and signs and wonders will add credibility to the Truth of God's Word. Revelation 11:6 says that the Two Witnesses (working through the 144,000) will perform miracles, and can strike the earth with every kind of plague as often as they want! BUT, (and this is an emphatic but) people will have to closely compare the testimony of those claiming to be God's messengers with the contents of the Bible, for Jesus said, **"For false Christs and false prophets will appear and perform great signs and miracles to deceive even the elect — if that were possible."** (Matthew 24:24) A careful examination is needed to distinguish the true from the false.

The devil is coming

The Bible predicts that Satan will physically appear as a dazzling being on the earth before the second coming of Jesus. (See 2 Corinthians 11:14 and 2 Thessalonians 2:1-9.) Satan is the man of lawlessness or sin. When he appears on Earth, he will eventually make senseless demands (lawlessness). His laws will have no regard for human rights or human dignity. At first, he will claim that he is God, and to demonstrate his assumed divinity, he will call fire down from heaven in full view of men. (Revelation 13:13) The physical appearing of Satan will not be a surprise to those people who understand Revelation, for the appearing of the devil occurs during the fifth trumpet. (Revelation 9:1-12; 17:8)

After Satan has appeared in various places on the earth for a few months, he will call on his followers, located in every nation, to take control. He will ask his followers to take up the sword and fight for the establishment of his kingdom. This war, described in Revelation 9:13-21, occurs during the sixth trumpet. This coming World War IV will be a repetition of the United States civil war that occurred last century, except the sixth trumpet war will involve every nation on earth.

Satan's followers intend to dominate their respective nations on behalf of the one they believe to be God! Millions upon millions will die as a result of this war. The Bible says in Revelation 9:16 that the number of troops will be 200,000,000. Currently, the entire world has less than 10 million soldiers in uniform. (We will investigate this horrible war later.) As a result of the carnage of this world war, wild animals will multiply rapidly. They will feed on the dead like the birds that feed on the wicked after the second coming. (Revelation 19:21)

Seven last plagues

But wait, there's more! The seven *last* plagues follow the seven *first* plagues (seven trumpets) and the seven last plagues also include the four judgments! These seven last plagues are described in Revelation 16, and all who receive the mark of the beast will receive these destructive judgments. The first judgment is a plague of sores that falls upon those receiving the mark of the beast. The second, third and fourth plagues deplete what food supplies remain. Famine will then be pandemic. Note that these plagues fall *only* on those who have rejected God's offer of salvation. Those who remain faithful to Jesus will not be affected by the plagues.

Jesus and the Father will appear in clouds of glory shortly before the seventh plague occurs. It may be a new thought for some people that the Father will attend the Son at the second coming. Notice the words of Jesus, **"...But I say unto you: In the future you will see the Son of Man**

sitting at the right hand of the Mighty One and coming on the clouds of heaven." (Matthew 26:64) Compare this text with Revelation 6:16,17: **"They called to mountains and rocks, 'Fall on us and hide us from the face of him who sits on the throne and from the wrath of the Lamb! For the great day of *their* wrath has come, and who can stand?' "**

Summary

The death and destruction of 1.4 billion people is beyond comprehension. Today (June, 1994), it seems like a fairy tale. But realize, God does nothing without purpose and cause. We have not explored the terrible things that people will do to one another during the trumpet judgments, nor have we explored what the prophecies say. So, reserve judgment on these matters. (These items will be addressed in subsequent chapters.) Revelation reveals that God's judgments come in two phases. The first phase is redemptive. That is, God awakens people so that they may realize the sinfulness of their course — and indeed, many will repent and be saved. The second phase of God's judgments will be utterly destructive. The seven last plagues only fall on those who choose to receive the mark of the beast.

Since I'm talking about death, an important point needs to be made. God does not see death as a terminus as we do. After all, He can speak the word and a dead man becomes a living man! (John 11:43) In fact, the Bible says that God does not look upon the dead as though they were dead, rather, He looks upon the dead as though they are *suspended* until the last day, the time of resurrection. Look at the following texts and see what you think! (Luke 20:38; Psalm 115:17; Ecclesiastes 9:5,6; John 6:39-54)

If you already know Jesus as your Savior, you have no reason to be afraid. The Psalmist wrote, **"Even though I walk through the valley of the shadow of death, I will fear no evil, for you are with me...."** (Psalm 23:4) If you have not given yourself to Jesus, surrender your life to Him today. Obey the teachings of Jesus and live by faith in His promises. Be willing and obedient to the prompting of the Holy Spirit and God will take care of you. Continue to search for God's truth; it will strengthen you. Earth's cup of iniquity is almost full. God is about to break His silence. The end of this old earth is just before us and the beginning of the New Earth lies just beyond.

Given the contents of this chapter, this statement may sound like a
contradiction in terms. Revelation contains a story of desperate love for
man. Jesus is anxious to save. But, most people are unable to understand
the character of God and His kingdom because we are so blighted by sin.
However, God will bring to the front of every person's conscience, the
reality of His character by sending His judgments. Into this turmoil, He
will send 144,000 messengers explaining the terms and conditions of salvation.
Yes, He wants everyone to be saved. But, many people will not listen, nor
give the respect due to Him. Perhaps some people will have to discover
their desperate need of a loving Savior in times of distress. What does it
say of man when God is left with nothing other than the outpouring of
His wrath to get our undivided attention?

Chapter 3

How God breaks His silence

Now that we know *why* the 14 judgments of God are coming, we need to understand *how* they come. Bible prophecy predicts a coming sequence of 14 events and there will be no question that God is doing exactly what He said He would do. His plans can be understood by anyone who wants to know what His coming actions are. Think about this: If the Bible record of coming events was obscure, how could God's children be certain that He is in control when the tribulation begins? This simple point will someday stand in direct opposition to the claims of skeptics. Indeed, you can be sure of this development: Many scoffers will deny that the judgments are deliberate Acts of God. Instead, they will say that these calamities are nothing more than nature's random curse.

A great earthquake

The first physical sign that marks the opening of the fourth seal will be a great earthquake that shakes the whole world. (**Note:** This earthquake is the first of four earthquakes predicted in Revelation.) This first earthquake signifies the end of God's patience with world conditions. In short, earth's cup of iniquity will spill over on that day. The first earthquake will not be an ordinary earthquake. This earthquake will be distinguished from all previous earthquakes in two ways:

1.   This earthquake will be accompanied by manifestations in the heavens and on earth. There will be rumblings deep in the earth, peals of thunder and lightning — simultaneously observed around the world.

2.   This earthquake will literally shake all of the nations of the world. The Richter scale will not be able to measure the power of this quake.

Then meteors fall

Shortly after the global earthquake, a shower of burning meteors will ignite unquenchable fires around the world. A meteoric hailstorm is not hard to accept once you know that our planet and solar system appear to be headed towards a dense region of an asteroid belt. An asteroid belt is a junk yard of orbiting cosmic debris, and the likelihood that Earth's gravity will attract some of the asteroids is almost certain. "It is inevitable," scientists say, "Earth will once again be hit by an asteroid large enough to cause mass extinctions..." (*National Geographic*, January 1985, page 47).

This disconcerting prediction, made a few years ago, now looks more ominous than ever before. Recent observations of new impact crater activity on the moon's surface and telescopic sightings of hundreds of meteorites burning up as they enter Earth's outer atmosphere may indicate Earth's closer proximity to the asteroid belt.

Scientists Clark Chapman and David Morrison startled 4,000 geoscientists at the American Geophysical Union in San Francisco in December 1989, saying, "In terms of risk, the significant danger (from asteroids) comes from impacts with global implications. Statistically, the greatest risk to each of us is (that) ...the impact could cause a global disruption of crops and/or food distribution systems, leading to widespread starvation and perhaps the death of most of the Earth's human population. We call this a civilization-threatening impact." At the time of the meeting in 1989, Dr. Chapman was a scientist at the Planetary Science Institute in Tucson, Arizona, and Dr. Morrison was chief of the Space Science Division at NASA's Ames Research Center in Mountain View, California.

These and other renowned scientists have known for years that asteroids and meteorites strike the earth and moon in predictable patterns. In fact, scientists observed a "near miss" when Asteroid 1989 FC (approximately 1,200 to 2,400 feet in diameter) missed Earth by a margin of only six hours. It was traveling at 46,000 mph. If it had hit Earth, Dr. Bevan French, an expert on large space objects at NASA's Solar System Exploration Division, calculated it would have released energy equivalent to 20,000 hydrogen bombs. If it had hit a metropolitan area such as Tokyo, Los Angeles or New York, millions would have died instantly. Fortunately, most meteorites that have impacted the earth in recent times have been small and have had no significant consequence.

Science takes another look

Since 1978, scientists have been seriously studying the possibility that "civilization-threatening impacts" have occurred on earth. This idea, widely controversial among geoscientists in the late 70's, has become serious because convincing evidence continues to accumulate from research centers around the world.

As a group, geoscientists are now convinced that our planet has experienced horrific impacts from large asteroids in the past. Because erosion constantly changes the face of the Earth, there is difficulty in detecting some large impact craters. Also, since 75% of Earth's surface is covered with water, the effects of asteroid impacts on the ocean are almost impossible to study.

At the present time there are about 130 known land-craters caused by asteroid or meteorite impacts. The three largest craters are found in Canada, South Africa and off the western coast of Mexico. Each crater has a diameter of about 120 - 150 miles. The largest known crater in the United States is about 18 miles wide and is located in Manson, Iowa. Even though craters are sprinkled over various continents, few are as distinct in appearance as Meteor Crater in Arizona. According to Richard A. F. Grieve, Ph.D., a scientist with the Geological Survey of Canada (*Scientific American*, April 1990), the "tiny" iron meteorite which caused Meteor Crater in Arizona was less than 200 feet in diameter and weighed approximately one million tons. It hit the earth traveling about 35,000 mph and released energy equivalent to the most powerful nuclear devices available today. Meteor Crater is about two-thirds of a mile wide and 640 feet deep.

The amount of damage caused by an impact is relative to the momentum and the direction of impact. Earth is traveling about 72,000 mph in its annual orbit about the sun. So, if a meteor traveling at 40,000 mph hit "head on" with Earth, the energy released would be equivalent to a collision at 112,000 mph! *National Geographic* magazine featured an impressive article titled "Extinctions" in its June 1989 edition, reported on the findings of scientists studying the effects of ancient asteroid impacts. The article still is timely because earth could be impacted by cosmic debris again.

Scientists, in the *National Geographic* article say that a scenario could go like this: "Giant meteorite strikes Earth, setting the planet afire. Volcanoes erupt, tsunamis crash into the continents. The sky grows dark for months, perhaps years. Unable to cope with the catastrophic changes in climate, countless species are wiped off the face of the planet" (page 686). The article goes on to suggest that great fires resulting from an asteroid would destroy crops, trees and vegetation. Even worse, wind storms created by the fires would destroy buildings hundreds of miles from the impact. Dust and smoke from the fires would find their way into the jet stream and block much of the sun's light thus altering the world's climate and the chances of human survival!

Will asteroids again impact Earth?

As stated earlier, what makes the prediction of scientists like Chapman, Morrison and others so plausible is that according to astronomers (see *National Geographic*, January 1985), our planet and solar system appear to be moving towards a large asteroid belt. Even worse, about 1,500 asteroids, each large enough to produce craters several miles in diameter, now intersect Earth's annual orbit around the sun! (Forty of these have been identified as extremely dangerous because they are traveling so fast.)

Scientists calculate that Asteroid 1989 FC will return and may be even closer to earth at some point in the near future! Will our gravitational field attract any of these celestial bodies? "Sooner or later, it is inevitable," scientists say. "Civilization-threatening" asteroids (rocks having a diameter of one to 10 miles) are so tiny in space that scientists rarely detect their presence until they are very close to Earth. In fact, the meteorite that missed earth in March 1989 was not detected until after it had passed by.

Hopes for the flawed $1.5 billion Hubbel telescope, put into orbit in 1990, were restored when astronauts repaired the giant eye in the sky. Now the question remains, will the orbiting telescope be able to detect approaching danger? The forthcoming impact on Jupiter in July, 1994, by fragmented comet "Shoemaker-Levy 9" should be recorded by the Hubbel, but what good is detection if a lethal-sized asteroid were attracted by the Earth's gravitational field? In all probability, nothing. Scientists speculate that nuclear missiles could blow an asteroid into little pieces or, even better, push an asteroid out of Earth's orbit — but this is only speculation.

Does Revelation predict asteroid impacts?

The predictions and warnings of scientists may be dismissed as scientific fantasy by many people. But what if these scientific predictions are the same conclusions being reached by those studying the prophecies of Revelation? The Bible does seem to predict the impact of "civilization-threatening asteroids and meteorites!" Revelation 8:7-11 describes a scenario that closely compares to what scientists anticipate from such impacts. Revelation symbolizes these events as "trumpets" because they are warnings, harbingers or announcements of the appearing of Jesus.

Great balls of fire

The first trumpet consists of a large meteoric shower of burning hail. Obviously, many people could die in a catastrophe of this type. Notice what Revelation says, **"The first angel sounded his trumpet, and there came hail and fire mixed with blood, and it was hurled down upon the earth. A third of the earth was burned up, a third of the trees were burned up, and all the green grass was burned up."** (Revelation 8:7)

Obviously, John saw great fires caused by burning hail. He saw a third of the Earth, a third of the trees and all the green grass burned up. What is the meaning of one-third? To appreciate this question, the reader should notice that the quantity of one-third is used 12 times throughout the seven trumpets:

1/3 of the earth will be burned up
1/3 of the trees will be burned up
1/3 of the sea will turn into blood
1/3 of the sea creatures will die
1/3 of the ships on the sea will sink
1/3 of the rivers and springs will become contaminated
1/3 of the light from the sun will be taken away
1/3 of the light from the moon will be taken away
1/3 of the light from the stars will be taken away
1/3 of the day will be without light
1/3 of the night will be without light
1/3 of the troops will be killed in the sixth trumpet war

So, what is the significance of one-third? The answer is generosity — for two-thirds are spared. In ancient times, when a nation refused to pay tribute (tax) to a more powerful king, it was not uncommon for the offended king to swarm down on the rebellious tribe and totally destroy it — men, women and children. However, if the king was generous, he would spare one-third from destruction. Notice this text: **"David also defeated the Moabites. He made them lie down on the ground and measured them off with a length of cord. Every two lengths of them were put to death, and the third length was allowed to live. So the Moabites became subject to David and brought tribute [tax]."** (2 Samuel 8:2)

In the same way, God tolerated the rebellion of Israel for many years, but when Israel's cup reached full measure, judgment day came. God swooped down on Israel using His servant Nebuchadnezzar, (Jeremiah 25:9) and destroyed two-thirds of Israel. Because He is a generous King, God spared one-third (the remnant), by scattering them throughout the world. God told Ezekiel, **"A third of your people will die of the plague or perish by famine inside you; a third will fall by the sword outside your walls; and a third I will scatter to the winds and pursue with drawn sword."** (Ezekiel 5:12)

Again, we see the balance of mercy in the days of Zechariah. God said, **" 'In the whole land,' declares the Lord, 'two-thirds will be struck down and perish; yet one-third will be left in it. This third I will bring into the fire; I will refine them like silver and test them like gold.**

They will call on my name and I will answer them; I will say, 'They are my people,' and they will say, 'The Lord is our God.' " (Zechariah 13:8,9)

So, the extensive use of one-third within the seven trumpets reveals God's generosity with a rebellious world. The trumpet-judgments are redemptive. If a generous king spared one-third of a rebellious nation in ancient times, what can be said of the King of Kings for sparing two-thirds of the elements mentioned in the seven trumpets? If God struck down two-thirds, certainly all life on this planet would perish in a few weeks!

Many people ask how the destructive thirds described in the trumpets connect with the destruction of one-fourth of the earth (mentioned in the fourth seal). The answer is that when all of the death and destruction of the trumpets is added together, a fourth of the earth is killed by God's judgments.

Calamitous impact on the sea

The second trumpet follows the first trumpet, and John describes a great impact upon the sea: **"The second angel sounded his trumpet, and something like a huge mountain, all ablaze, was thrown into the sea. A third of the sea turned into blood, a third of the living creatures in the sea died, and a third of the ships were destroyed."** (Revelation 8:8,9)

This scene apparently describes a large asteroid, the size of a mountain, hitting the sea. If an asteroid, one mile in diameter, was sitting upon the surface of the Earth, it would be 5,280 feet high. So, the term "mountain" is most appropriate for a huge rock or asteroid. John's description of an asteroid impact upon the sea is identical with scientific predictions. For example, the resulting tidal wave would destroy ships for hundreds of miles in every direction — even those docked in seaports far away. According to scientists at the University of California, the asteroid would be so hot that it would make a large part of the ocean water anoxic (oxygen deficient) by simply boiling the oxygen out of a large area of the sea. The temperature of the water would also dramatically rise, thus killing whatever creature life was left. Then, the warm, anoxic water would provide a perfect environment for the growth of red algae or what is known as red tide.

John said the sea turned to blood. This appropriately describes the appearance of red algae, which thrives in oxygen deficient water!

Horrific impact on land

John describes the third trumpet as a great star that impacts the Earth. **"The third angel sounded his trumpet, and a great star, blazing like a torch, fell from the sky on a third of the rivers and on the springs of water — the name of the star is Wormwood. A third of the waters turned bitter, and many people died from the waters that had become bitter."** (Revelation 8:10,11)

Many prophecy experts insist on a symbolic interpretation of these verses because they do not believe these things will literally happen. However, two compelling reasons eliminate the possibility of symbolic interpretation. First, each event described by John is physically consistent with the literal outcome he gives; second, if these texts were symbolic, where is the explanation or interpretation of these symbols within the Bible? (Remember the third rule of interpretation? See page 8.)

Suppose a large star (asteroid), blazing like a torch, were to impact one of Earth's seven continents. What would be the consequences? Ground waves would sheer water wells and sewer lines for hundreds of miles in all directions. Earthquakes and tremors would occur for many days as enormous tectonic forces beneath the surface of the earth adjust to the impact. Remember, a large asteroid impact would release the energy of thousands of nuclear bombs. The end result is that drinking water would become contaminated because broken sewer systems and toxic waste buried in landfills would enter subterranean aquifers. Millions of people in large cities would drink the contaminated water, and sickness would be followed by death. Notice again that Revelation 8:10,11 predicts many people will die from drinking bitter water that has become unsafe as the direct consequence of a star hitting the Earth!

Sun, moon and stars darkened

The fourth trumpet follows the first three trumpets. The sun, moon and stars turn dark. Perhaps the darkness that fell across the northwestern part of the United States during the Mount St. Helens eruption in 1980, is a good example of what John saw. Although Revelation does not say why the sun, moon and stars turn dark, this result would be consistent with volcanic eruptions. If we add the effects of a giant earthquake, a meteoric storm of burning hail and two asteroid impacts together, the fragile balance of Earth's tectonic plates could be disrupted. To release the enormous energy, volcanoes could erupt and belch magma and ash in a series of explosions that would dwarf the blasts of Mount St. Helens and Mount Pinatubo in the Philippines.

The first three trumpets send megatons of dust, soot and debris into the atmosphere. Chains of volcanic eruptions (around the Ring of Fire) belch more dust in the form of volcanic ash, potentially causing extended darkness around the world. Millions of burning acres and resulting windstorms will insure that the jet stream is affected. One ounce of soot absorbs 25,000 times the sunlight that one ounce of dust absorbs! Given this physical fact, it is not hard to see how a band of darkness could encircle of the Earth.

Same conclusions and some predictions

What makes the first four trumpets so uncanny is that scientists and Bible students are not only arriving at the same conclusions — that asteroids and meteorites will impact earth — but they are also surprised by the consistent harmony of results. Will earth be pummelled by rocks raining from heaven? More and more scientists are convinced it is inevitable, and so are students of Revelation.

As mentioned before, I anticipate that the meteor showers of the first trumpet will occur in 1994 or 1995. Will we soon see these great demonstrations of God's anger? I believe so. I believe God has two asteroids out there ready for Earth. I also believe that 1994 or 1995 could be the time of the rendezvous.

In God we trust?

God knows the end from the beginning. Therefore, 2,000 years ago He had Revelation written in such a way that when the time of the end came, the final generation on earth would know that it is the last generation. Also, God gave us His Word that we would have hope, comfort and patience. When God breaks His silence, the world's financial systems will collapse. The wonderful infrastructures we depend on for every aspect of life will be gone. In this coming atmosphere of terror, fear and anxiety, God will open the minds of men and women to see His moment-by-moment interest in them. The response will be varied. Millions will become despondent and curse God — even to the point of taking their own lives — while others will zealously turn religious as a means of saving themselves. Those who know how to live by faith will trust in God for survival and salvation. They will share with others the purpose of God's visitations.

And now, a vitally important point. Not only does Revelation predict the impact of asteroids and meteorites and global darkness, but it also explains the response of man. You cannot afford to miss this part of the story. So, stay tuned. You need to know what your leaders are going to do.

Chapter 4

Asteroid impact immediately changes life

If you find the interpretation of the first four trumpets in the previous chapter to be reasonable, and the impact models by scientists within reason, Revelation will provide a very compelling story. The story is not, I repeat, is not disconnected from the international backdrop that exists when the meteors and asteroids collide with our planet. Revelation's story not only predicts the horrific events that immediately change life on Earth, but it also reveals the reactions of religious and political powers at the time the events occur! To understand the actions and reactions of world leaders, consider this simple scenario of Earth's condition after the first four trumpets.

Nature's dilemma

Scientists predict that wildfires set by a meteor shower could last for months. With megatons of ejecta and ash from the fires circulating in the atmosphere, global darkness would compound a miserable problem. Combine the destruction of meteoric firestorms with two large asteroid impacts, and any optimist would doubt the possibility of survival on Earth.

Food crops surviving the wildfires would not likely receive enough light to reach maturity because the sun's light will not shine through clouds of ash and soot. This is especially true of food crops, such as corn, which require 100+ days of sunlight to reach maturity. That food will become scarce is an understatement. (In 1994, the world's stockpile of food is less than 60 days.) The rain that falls would be so acidic that it may be lethal for plant and animal life, even though it could fall hundreds of miles away from the actual impact site. In short, Earth's delicate ecosphere of life will be damaged beyond repair!

This is why Chapman, Morrison and other scientists warn that an asteroid could produce a "civilization-threatening impact." Although Revelation's story reveals what people will do after the first four trumpets, it also gives a few clues about the physical conditions on earth during that time. For example, Revelation 11:6 indicates that certain places on earth will go without rain for three years. Also, famine is one of the judgments mentioned in the fourth seal. (Revelation 6:7,8) Further, Revelation 8:11 says that many people will die from drinking contaminated water.

Because medical malpractice litigation has put many vaccine producers out of business, there will be gross shortages of life-saving vaccines. Disease will become rampant and survival will be questionable in every person's mind. Jesus said, **"For then there will be great distress, unequaled from the beginning of the world until now — and never to be equaled again. If those days had not been cut short, no one would survive, but for the sake of the elect those days will be shortened."** (Matthew 24:21,22)

Global economic ruin

What will happen to Earth's global economy if the predictions of the scientists and our interpretation of the first four trumpets of Revelation are true?

1. Suppose the meteoric showers of burning hail of the first trumpet ignite great forest fires all over the world. In just a few days a critical resource would be destroyed that cannot be replenished in decades. Trees are used for the production of paper, building materials and many, many other items, but most of all, trees produce oxygen. If you add millions of acres in wheat, corn and other food crops to the burning inferno, you can see how respiratory problems could kill millions of livestock and people. Mass graves will be everywhere. Food will become as scarce as gold. Never in the history of the world will the index of human suffering reach this level. (Matthew 24:21,22)

2. Suppose one-third of the ships are sent to the bottom of the ocean by a tidal wave produced by an asteroid impact. Millions of barrels of oil in super-tankers will be spilled. Billions of dollars in cargo from Japan, Russia, America and other countries will rest on the bottom of the ocean. Countries that heavily depend on oil and food supplies arriving by sea will experience immediate shortages of all kinds. Large seaports will be washed away, and thousands, perhaps millions of people will drown. Large insurance companies will go bankrupt leaving investment banking in the world's stock markets in total chaos. The domino effect on the economy of all nations will be beyond calculation.

3. Great cities along the seaboard will be totally destroyed by tidal waves exceeding 1,000 feet in height. If an asteroid, one mile in diameter, hits an ocean — much of the coastline could be destroyed. Entire islands could be washed away! Even worse, many countries depend on their fertile coast lands for valuable food crops. The destruction of these areas would bring dire circumstances to every human being, especially when you consider that many people keep less than one week's food supply on hand. Perhaps this kind of speculation sounds like a fairy tale, but Luke talks about the fury of the ocean before the coming of Jesus saying, **"There will be signs in the sun, moon and stars. On the earth, nations will be in anguish and perplexity at the roaring and tossing of the sea. Men will faint from terror, apprehensive of what is coming on the world...."** (Luke 21:25,26)

4. Compound the destruction of our nation's food basket with the horror of contaminated drinking water everywhere, and the situation grows so desperate that a person would wonder if life can go on at all. Desperate circumstances call for extreme efforts. To stabilize the situation, governments will respond quickly. First, they will, of necessity enact contingency or emergency constitutions. This means that martial law will be implemented to prevent anarchy and the total breakdown of government. Stringent laws will be implemented and people will have no choice but to acquiesce. Individual rights will be cancelled. The price for sin is always great — even upon the innocent.

5.   Rationing will be implemented to prevent total anarchy. People, full of fear, will do everything they can to obtain food and medicine. Controls on buying and selling will become necessary since every survivor needs a basic number of items to sustain life itself. Few will argue with the drastic economic methods enacted for survival. As days turn into weeks and weeks into months, people will give in to despair. Hope for recovery will dim. On every point of the compass there will be destruction and suffering beyond description. All the people of earth will be in a state of shock. The living will envy the dead.

What does God want?

The story that follows is as dramatic as the story of the first four trumpets! In a sentence, the administration of life on planet Earth as we now know it will be changed overnight. Pandemonium, confusion, fear, depression, stupor and distress will rule the day. Out of suffering certain questions always rise: "Why did God allow this? Why did He do this? What does He want?"

According to Revelation, a great transformation will take place all over the world as a result of the meteor and asteroid impacts. The most remarkable change in America will be a great surge of national repentance. Currently, only 39% of Americans attend church regularly. This percentage will change overnight. Religion will become a priority and evangelicals will lead the nation — almost overnight — into a religious revolution.

Religious revolution

Clergy from all religious systems will come forward with a straightforward explanation of God's judgments. They will quickly adjust their lame interpretations to fit the situation. (Why didn't they proclaim these things *before* they happened since they claim to understand the Bible?) They will also claim to have the solution for stopping the judgments of God. They will say, "These Acts of God have come because we have forgotten our Creator." The cry, "Man has forgotten God," will be heard around the world. Clerics of all faiths will agree saying, "We must repent of our great sins and appease God or we will be totally destroyed."

Jewish, Catholic and Protestant leaders will turn to the Old Testament to prove their point, for there is abundant scripture supporting the idea that God sends judgments upon people when they become evil. They will quote from Old Testament chapters such as Daniel 9; Isaiah 24, 25; Ezekiel 7; and Jeremiah 25.

As people begin to link the devastations of the four trumpets to the idea that God is displeased with the human race, one question will be on everyone's mind: "What must we do to appease God?" Even though different solutions will be offered in different lands, a common theme will develop around the world. Revelation indicates there will be a global rush to appease God. Laws will be implemented in every land that demand we respect the laws of God or perish.

Number one question

There are several different religious systems on earth and each one worships its God in a different way. Is there *one* right way to worship God? Mentally step out into space and look down on earth for a moment. Moslems believe that God is pleased when people obey the teachings of Mohammed. Catholics believe that God is pleased when people obey the pope and the laws of the church. Protestants, Jews, Hindus and others have differing ideas on what pleases God. Which religious system is right? Does God really care how we worship Him as long as we worship Him? This question is about to become the number one question on Earth. In today's context, the question appears to be rhetorical, but when God's anger is felt by billions of people, this question will become paramount.

Desperate circumstances quickly unite people when they focus on a common problem or solution. (The war between Iraq and the United Nations' coalition of 29 nations led by the United States in 1990 proved this point.) Shortly after the trumpets begin, Revelation predicts the world will participate in the rapid development of a global religious coalition. Instead of nations fighting and quarreling among themselves over lesser things like power, land or money, the judgments of God will propel religious leaders into a significant leadership role comprised of confused people. Prompted by terror, controlled by fear and trying to be significant, clerics will call for drastic measures to appease God so His judgments will cease. Because the destruction of the first four trumpets is global, the union of religious leaders will be global.

The wrath of God

A great change will occur overnight in the way people think about God. Most Christians talk about God's love, His great salvation and forgiveness, but little is said about the things that make Him angry. Many Christians even deny that God has wrath! Consequently, when His judgments begin to fall, many Christians will be at a loss to reconcile these "Acts of God" with their assumed knowledge of God. The result will be great fear and terror.

It is not difficult for God to frighten people. He only needs to tamper with things that make us feel secure to get our attention. When lives and property are destroyed, the survivors tend to renew their acquaintance with God. Like Israel of old, all nations will tremble with fear before Almighty God during the days of His visitation. (Exodus 20:18-21) The solution to pleasing or appeasing God — so that His destruction of earth will stop — will appear simple on the surface. Religious leaders will cry out, "Submit to the authority of God." But how does a person worship the God of Heaven so that His wrath is satisfied? (Remember, one of the five doctrinal pillars in this story is the truth about the worship of God.)

Revelation explains what God wants. John saw a message going throughout the world saying, **"Fear God and give him glory, because the hour of his judgment has come. Worship him who made the heavens, the earth, the sea and the springs of water."** (Revelation 14:7) Notice that the last sentence of this verse itemizes the four things affected by the first four trumpets! Religious people, the world over, will quickly agree *why* the judgments are falling, and *what* they are, but *how* to implement a solution that will please God will become a global nightmare! The nightmare is because the judgments of God will be common upon all people; but, there are different religions on the earth and each claims that its way is the *only* right way to worship God.

(For the rest of this chapter, remember that you are watching this scenario unfold on the earth from your position in outer space.)

Laws enforcing worship

Revelation predicts that people the world over will respond to the devastation of the trumpets by enforcing laws that demand the worship of God. However, there will be no consistency between the laws; instead, there will be great confusion. Catholics and Protestants will seek laws that agree with their theology, Jews will make laws agreeing with their doctrine, Moslems will want laws respecting their beliefs in Allah, and other bodies will demand similar laws. Notice the problem that occurs with diverse religions. How can diverse religions appease one God? Is He a God of many religions?

To address global diversity, Revelation states that a global coalition of religious representatives will quickly form. This coalition will try to solve the problem of diverse views about God. This coming global union is called "Babylon" in the Bible because Babylon symbolizes confusion.

Why does Babylon form?

Well-meaning religious people will stampede the political processes of their respective countries after the trumpets begin, and the legislated results will be very confusing, severe and most distressing. In every nation, religious leaders will demand laws to end the "reign of sin" so that God may be appeased and the judgments stopped. Politicians will be powerless to stop the increase of religious sentiment and laws will be enacted overnight.

Compare Daniel 3 with Revelation 13 and you will find that modern Babylon's story parallels the experience of ancient Babylon. Modern Babylon, like ancient Babylon, will be made up of many religions, cultures and nationalities. When the devil himself, the coming king of modern Babylon, physically appears on earth during the fifth trumpet, he will use his miracle working powers to convince people that he is God. Obviously, this coming demonic god-man will rule over Babylon. The ultimate purpose behind his deceit is to unite as many people as possible into a one-world religion and then implement his one-world order. Satan will eventually obtain a death penalty for those people who will refuse to meet his demands. At that time, the followers of Jesus will be exposed because they refuse to join ranks with the devil and receive his tattoo, the mark of the lamb-like beast.

The mark of the beast is easy to identify; a person does not need to be a theologian to understand the mark. It will either be a tattoo placed on the right hand showing the literal number 666 or it will be the name of the devil tattooed on the forehead. (Revelation 13:17,18) It is that simple. Those who join the devil's forces will have to wear either the name of the devil on their forehead or the number on the right hand. Everybody knows that 666 is evil. Yet, billions will choose it rather than worship God. This will be true in all regions of the world, including China, India, Europe, Russia, America and Borneo. The mark will be visible to all, because no one will be allowed to buy or sell without it. The mark will be implemented upon humanity during the sixth trumpet.

One world — one God — many religions

One organization on earth stands head and shoulders above all others in terms of diplomatic ties with religious and political leaders all over the world. It is the papacy. The Roman Catholic Church has steadily secured diplomatic connections with almost every segment of Earth's population since John Paul II became Pope in 1978.

When the trumpets begin, the pope will move quickly to orchestrate a "World Congress" of religious and political bodies. This congress is the organization called Babylon. Perhaps the United Nations will also be a vehicle for such an organization. But understand, the glue that will bond the elements of the world together will not be politics. It will be immediate concerns about God and His anger. Religious differences will be hastily compromised and efforts to appease God will begin on a global scale. Yet, a global solution will remain elusive. The problem is this: "How does God want all of the earth to worship Him?" Moslems, Jews, Catholics, Hindus, Protestants and other religious organizations will have fundamentally different answers. This dilemma will be solved during the fifth trumpet, when the devil himself appears on earth claiming to be God. The devil will exalt himself above all religions, and he will unite the world into one religion. More will be said about this in a following chapter.

Consider the question

Think about this for a moment. Sincere people all over the earth worship God according to what they believe is true worship, and the Bible says that God accepts such worship. According to Romans 2, John 4 and Acts 10:35, God accepts the worship of all people on earth if they worship Him in spirit and in truth. This means that if anyone worships God with a humble and obedient spirit according to all the truth they know, then God, ever generous and merciful, accepts their worship as genuine.

The human race, however, is not living up to the spirit and truth of what we know to be right! Legislators should realize by now that *laws do not make people good.* Rather, laws direct good people and they provide a means for punishing law breakers. Laws are only useful if people live by them. When personal decency and integrity becomes nonexistent in the majority of people, then evil, violence and suffering escalate. Nothing rouses the anger of God more than immorality and violence, because the quality of life for generations to come is ruined by these cancers. History is full of sad examples. Destructive behavior and decadence overtake a nation whenever its people forget their individual accountability to their Creator. This is why God, at various times and in different ways, broke His silence. Whenever sin fills the cup, God breaks His silence. (Proverbs 6:16-19)

The gospel truth

Here is an interesting paradox. Lawless behavior is everywhere. Political leaders recognize that government structures can only remain intact if there is law and order. The Bible states that when world leaders begin pleading for world order, world peace and safety, God will break His silence. According to 1 Thessalonians 5:3, this day must be near. Paul wrote: **"While people are saying, 'Peace and safety,' destruction will come on them suddenly, as labor pains on a pregnant woman, and they will not escape."**

The seven trumpets of Revelation are not totally destructive, or the world would immediately perish. This is why John uses the "one-third" portion to explain how the elements are harmed. The first four trumpets are designed to literally arrest the attention of 5.6 billion people, so that all will listen to the gospel and learn what God wants. In other words, the world must hear the unvarnished truth about God and His claims upon man. To accomplish this task, God will empower 144,000 people to proclaim the everlasting gospel. These individuals will explain the appropriate way to glorify God and they will show how it is an integral part of the everlasting gospel.

The message of the 144,000 will oppose the efforts of the religious leaders of Babylon. Since the everlasting gospel contains specific instructions on worship, a great controversy will arise. What is the acceptable way to worship Almighty God? Everyone has to know the truth on this matter. This is why Jesus said the gospel must go to every nation and to every person before the end comes. (Matthew 24:14)

The eternal gospel reveals what God wants of us, and one of the primary elements of the eternal gospel is worship. Questions regarding worship will cause an enormous controversy which will soon engulf every person on Earth. Each of the world's religious systems claims to have the truth about God and in an effort to please God, each political body will enact laws respecting the prevailing religious belief of its people. Moslems in Iran will enact compulsory laws to reverence Allah on Friday. Catholics and Protestants will enact Sunday laws — claiming that God requires worship on Sunday. Jews and other religious groups will also enact laws regarding respect for God in their lands on certain days. The problem, according to Revelation, is that these coming laws will be contrary to the law of God — which is the legal basis for His wrath in the first place!

God does not accept the worship of human beings if they knowingly reject His commands. This issue will fuel an enormous controversy among the people of earth at a time when the religious and political leaders of the world are desperately trying to appease God. Revelation predicts that Babylon will enact laws regarding worship, and most of the world will submit to man-made laws rather than obey the law of God. John wrote, **"All inhabitants of the earth will worship the beast (Babylon) — all whose names have not been written in the book of life belonging to the Lamb that was slain from the creation of the world."** (Revelation 13:8)

Chapter 5

Satan appears in person

The first four trumpets have reduced Planet Earth to complete chaos. Planet Earth has received a deadly blow. Now, the next event described in Revelation is the fifth trumpet. The fifth trumpet reveals that the devil himself will physically appear on earth after the "dust settles" from the asteroid impacts. He may first appear in the Middle East, perhaps Jerusalem. The Bible does not say, but many orthodox Jews anticipate the imminent arrival of Messiah to deliver them from their enemies. Their hopes for the coming Messiah would provide an easy platform for deception that Satan could use to a great advantage, especially since many Christians believe the Jews are still God's chosen people. In addition to the Jews' expectation of the coming Messiah, the Arabs also believe a Deliverer will soon appear. So, it is not hard to see why the Middle East could be an excellent geographical target for Satan!

When Satan first appears, he will be a glorious being and he will claim to be the "Savior of the World." At that moment in time, the world will be in a most vulnerable position. The cry for help will be everywhere and the enemy of mankind will demonstrate great sympathy for human suffering. To make his deception even more secure, he will perform great and wonderful miracles of blessing.

Who is the devil?

According to the Bible, the devil once had an exalted name. His name was Lucifer — which means "light bearer." A quick review of Isaiah 14:12-17 and Ezekiel 28:12-18 reveals that Lucifer was once a mighty angel in Heaven. Apparently, he became proud and vain and ultimately became dissatisfied with the way God was running the universe. Lucifer sowed seeds of disaffection among the angels which led to a great rebellion in Heaven. According to Revelation 12, Satan and his angels were cast out of Heaven. Jesus told His disciples, **"I saw Satan fall like lightning from heaven."** (Luke 10:18)

Angry and bitter with his defeat, Lucifer focused his hostility toward the ruination of God's special handiwork — planet Earth. He went to the Garden of Eden and led Adam and Eve to disobey God. The devil did not stop with our first parents. Cain, the firstborn of Adam and Eve, became a murderer. As time went by, earth became so defiled as a result of Satan's influence, that God was grieved that He had even made man! (Genesis 6) So God washed the earth clean of sin with a flood of water, sparing just eight people — Noah and his family. Unfortunately, the flood only slowed the devil down for a season. Peter tells us the devil is still alive and goes about seeking whom he may devour! (1 Peter 5:8,9)

Satan allowed to live

So, why did God allow the devil to live? Why didn't He put Satan and his angels out of existence and spare earth all the grief? The answer is both simple and profound.

1. If God had immediately zapped Lucifer and the angels who disagreed with Him, what kind of God would He be? He would be nothing more than a dictator — a selfish and self-promoting God! Think about this: If God quickly exterminates anyone who disagrees with Him, He would be the biggest bully in the universe. Wouldn't He?
2. God, having infinite wisdom, knows that sin should be allowed a brief period of existence (speaking in terms of eternity) so that all His universe can see the consequences of sin. By allowing rebellion to exist for a time, everyone (including Satan and his angels) can see for themselves that God's principles of government are best — not because God says His ways are best — but rather, because they have been demonstrated to be righteous.

3.   God freely gives the power of choice to each created being. His
        subjects do not have to obey Him. They do not have to love Him.
        They do not have to respond to His goodness or generosity. Lucifer
        and his angels have proven this. They have lived long enough to
        demonstrate the consequences of their own choosing. Adam and Eve
        also proved that they had the power of choice by disobeying God.
        They were given the power of choice and they chose to experience
        the dire consequences of sin. Time has proved that there is no quality
        of life in rebellion against God. True, sin may seem to offer pleasure
        and excitement for a *short* season, but it extracts a far greater price
        than the value of a cheap thrill. Sin takes us farther than we want
        to go, and sin costs us more than we want to pay. No matter how
        well Satan disguises sin, **"the wages of sin is death."** (Romans
        6:23)
4.   God chose to keep Lucifer and his angels alive for awhile, even
        though He foreknew the consequences. Therefore, God, at great
        expense, provided a plan of salvation for all the people who would
        live on Earth. He loved the people of the world so much that He
        gave us the life of His only Son. Jesus was willing to come and
        die for man so that the penalty for sin could be paid! God Himself
        has paid a much greater price for the existence of sin than any
        human being will ever know!

So, the conflict between Jesus and Lucifer has been in progress on
earth for nearly 6,000 years. Today, both still strive to win the affections
of people. I believe this struggle will come to a climax before this
decade ends.

Out of the bottomless pit

Revelation says the devil is going to enter the realm of our senses and
will physically appear before our eyes. This process is predicted in Revelation
9 where the devil is portrayed as coming out of the abyss or bottomless
pit! To appreciate the prediction and the meaning of John's language, we
need to understand a little about ancient history.

People living during Bible times thought the earth was flat, much like a
large plate or basin. To them, the ocean was flat. Having limited knowledge

about the law of gravity, they reasoned that the earth must be basin-like. They believed the ocean would "drain away" if the world was spherical. Because the ancients thought the world was flat, they believed a bottomless pit would be created if a person dug a hole all the way through the basin of the earth. Without a bottom, the pit would be a very dangerous place into which a person could fall and never be seen again. Understanding John's mindset helps us understand the Biblical term "bottomless pit" or "abyss."

The transliteration of the Greek word *abussos* in English is "abyss." Whether it is called "bottomless pit" or "abyss," the idea is identical. In Bible times, the term "bottomless pit" represented the source or origin of evil things. People believed that demons lived in caves and holes which had no bottom or end to them. The term "abyss" or "bottomless pit" is used several times in Revelation. When God revealed last-day events to John in A.D. 95, God used imagery that John was familiar with to represent things that would happen at the end of time. John saw the devil and his angels ascend out of a bottomless pit and John refers to this event in several places in Revelation. Many people are surprised to learn that Revelation predicts that Satan will physically appear on earth for a period of time just before the coming of Jesus! Revelation not only tells us when, but it also tells us why!

The fifth trumpet

God only allows the devil to physically appear *after* a significant part of the world has heard the gospel. Satan is allowed to appear because most of earth has already heard and rejected the gospel as proclaimed by the 144,000. Therefore, God releases and empowers the devil to rule over those who refused to recognize Him as the Almighty. This is an interesting point about the Great Tribulation: Each man will have a master, either by his choice or by force. Who will it be? The time periods in Revelation suggest that the devil will appear about two years after the fourth trumpet sounds.

This occurs when the fifth trumpet of Revelation 9:1-11 begins and the bottomless pit is "unlocked." God shows John something that looks like a great swarm of locusts coming up out of the earth. As the swarm draws closer to him, John can see that they look like riders on horses. Directing the riders is an angel king whose name in Hebrew is Abaddon and in Greek, is Apollyon. Both names mean the same thing: "destroyer."

The language of Revelation 9:1-11 is parallel to Joel 2:1-11. Joel describes the coming of the Lord with His mighty host of angels. Joel describes the scene as a great swarm of horses prepared for battle. John, in Revelation, uses the same language as Joel to describe what he sees, except the swarm originates in the bottomless pit.

The release of Satan and his angels from the bottomless pit reveals three important things. First, Satan will not come in the clouds of glory *exactly* like Jesus. Although Satan will do everything in his power to imitate Jesus' second coming, God limits the deception of the devil. Satan will appear to come down from the clouds in various places. This is why Jesus said, **"At that time if anyone says to you, 'Look, here is the Christ!' or, 'There he is!' do not believe it."** (Matthew 24:23) Second, God does not allow Satan to physically appear on earth until the first four trumpets have sounded. Last, the physical appearing of the devil is designed by God to force everyone into a firm decision. The door of salvation is still open for anyone who might repent of their rebellion and turn to God.

According to Revelation 9, for the first five months after Satan and his evil angels appear, they will torment "unsaved" people. Just how the torment is inflicted and what the torment is, is not clear from scripture. What is known is that the torment will hurt like a scorpion sting. Those people who are afflicted will long to die, but they will actually survive the ordeal.

An angel of light

When Satan appears, he will so dazzle the people of earth with his glory that many will believe his claims to be God on the basis of appearance alone. Paul says, **"...for Satan himself masquerades as an angel of light."** (2 Corinthians 11:14) Revelation states that when Satan appears, he will be so dazzling and glorious that most people will be awe-struck when they actually see him! **"...The inhabitants of the earth whose names have not been written in the book of life from the creation of the world will be *astonished* when they see the beast...."** (Revelation 17:8, Italics added.)

Satan works miracles, signs and wonders

Satan's first work after appearing "in the flesh" as a glorious god-man will
be to convince the world that he is divine — that he is actually God. Paul
warns, **"Don't let anyone deceive you in any way, for that day (the
second coming) will not come until the rebellion occurs and the man
of lawlessness is revealed, the man doomed to destruction. He opposes
and exalts himself over everything that is called God or is worshiped,
and even sets himself up in God's temple, proclaiming himself to be
God. ...The coming of the lawless one will be in accordance with the
work of Satan displayed in all kinds of counterfeit miracles, signs and
wonders, and in every sort of evil that deceives those who are perishing.
They perish because they refused to love the truth and so be saved."**
(2 Thessalonians 2:3,4,9,10)

Calls fire down out of heaven

The one miracle that Satan will use above all others to convince doubting
people that he is God, will be his ability to call fire down out of heaven
at will! This "proof of divinity" will make his deceptions secure for many,
many people. John says, **"And he performed great and miraculous signs,
even causing fire to come down from heaven to earth in full view of
men. Because of the signs he was given power to do on behalf of the
first beast, he deceived the inhabitants of the earth...."** (Revelation
13:13,14)

John describes the appearing of Satan as a "lamb-like" beast. The intended
contrast is obvious, for in Revelation, Jesus is referred to as "The Lamb"
more than 29 times. Because the devil masquerades as Jesus, John describes
Satan as a "lamb-like" beast. John also warns that he will make every
effort to deceive the world.

The scene reviewed

For you to appreciate the grandest deception ever to occur on earth, we
have to review the circumstances existing throughout the world when the
devil appears. When Satan appears, every quadrant of earth has experienced

massive destruction and suffering as a result of the first four trumpets. Earth's skies have been dark for a time, and billions of people (that's billions) have grown hopeless. The death toll is numberless, and tens of thousands of people have died every day from famine and disease. People are filled with despair, and clerics continue to lament that people must repent and worship God so that His anger will subside. Religious persecution and intolerance is everywhere because Babylon is determined to settle the issue. The question, "What must we do to please God so that He will stop the suffering?", is foremost in the minds of all people at that time.

Into this nightmare the devil gloriously appears. Satan will use great displays of signs and wonders to deceive, if possible, the very elect. His purpose has always been to destroy this world and when his day of opportunity comes, it will be a splendid moment to fulfill this ambition. The devil then turns the majority of the world away from hearing and believing the gospel, and in time, will force the world's people into false worship on pain of death! Revelation 13:15 says, **"He, [Satan]... caused all who refused to worship the image to be killed."**

The image or death

What is the image of the beast? The image of the beast is the consolidation of the world's religions into one global religion. When Catholics, Jews, Protestants, Moslems and Hindus believe that Satan is actually God, they will be willing to do whatever he demands. To make people believe that he is God, Satan will display his marvelous powers. At the same time, his demonic angels will severely torment a large number of "unsaved" people. The devil will then blame the affliction of the "wicked" upon the 144,000 who are proclaiming the gospel of Jesus. How believable will his claim be? His claim will be most plausible since the 144,000 have already demonstrated supernatural powers. (Revelation 11:6) Therefore, the devil's accusation will have considerable credibility and wicked people will naturally believe him. So, the wicked will vent their hostility on God's people by killing them — all the while thinking that they are doing their man-god (the devil) a service! (John 16:2)

A day of testing

The seven trumpets are specifically designed to awaken the world to the return of Jesus. If anyone wishes to receive salvation during this time-period, he or she must worship the Creator of the heavens, earth, the sea and springs of water. The word worship simply means "to render obedience." Now, every Christian should know that man *is not saved* by obedience, for the Bible states that we are saved by faith. (Ephesians 2:8,9) So, the primary purpose of the Great Tribulation is to test faith. God is going to test the faith of all men and women by setting before us a life or death test. In this context, each person's faith will be revealed through obedience! Those choosing to submit to the laws of man — will reject God's sovereign authority. Those choosing to submit to the laws of God — will reject man's effort to dictate how God is to be worshiped. It is interesting that the penalty for rejecting either God's laws or man's laws is death. Read Daniel 3 and Daniel 6 for two stories that demonstrate the ultimate test of faith.

The irony of this story is: The 144,000 will proclaim that all must obey God's law at a time when Babylon is *demanding the same thing!* Remember, clerics from all religious systems throughout the world will be proclaiming with a united voice "God has sent these judgments upon earth because we are sinful." They will also say that God must be appeased before His judgments will cease. They will proclaim that if the nations of earth do not appease God soon, He will ultimately destroy all of us. As a result, the religious leaders of Babylon will demand the enforcement of laws requiring obedience to God. Moslems will appeal to the Koran for authority about the worship of God; Jews will appeal to the Talmud, the Mishna and the Torah; and Catholics will look to the pope and the catechism for directions on worship. To what authority will Protestants appeal — the Bible?

A holy day mystery

God has clearly expressed in the Bible how His subjects are to worship Him. This is not a matter left to human design. Unfortunately, the devil, during the past 6,000 years, has obscured God's truth and implemented many false religions around the world. During this time, Babylon (Satan's union of world religions) will face a peculiar problem. Each religious system demands the worship of *one* God in different ways! For example, Moslems regard Friday as a holy day, the Jews regard Saturday, and Christians regard Sunday! Remember, Revelation 13:8 says, **"All inhabitants of the earth will worship the beast [Babylon, which has seven heads and ten horns] — all whose names have not been written in the book of life belonging to the Lamb that was slain...."** Is there a right way and a wrong way to worship God? Is God specific about how we must worship Him? Yes.

The story of Cain and Abel illustrates the primary difference between false and true worship. Both worshiped. Both built altars. Abel worshiped God by obediently sacrificing a lamb according to God's instruction. Cain did as *he* thought best. In effect, Cain told God how He was to be worshiped. Thus, Cain exalted himself above God and God refused to recognize his offering. (Genesis 4:1-16)

Cain became violently angry and slew his brother. Why? John warns, **"Do not be like Cain, who belonged to the evil one and murdered his brother. And why did he murder him? Because his own actions were evil and his brother's were righteous. Do not be surprised, my brothers, if the world hates you."** (1 John 3:12,13) John says Cain's act of worship was evil! Indeed, it was blasphemous, for Cain took the prerogative of God. *He thought he could tell God how He should be worshiped!* Think about this. If a created being can tell his Creator how or when He is to be worshiped, then the created being has authority over the Creator. How can a human being presume such a thing?

The crux of the matter is this. God accepts our worship if we worship Him in spirit and in truth; that is, if we worship God according to all we know to be true. The eternal gospel that goes to every nation, kindred, tongue and people contains information about the worship of the God that will be *new* to most people. The first angel's message says loudly, "Fear God... and worship the Creator." The reason the first angel's message begins in this manner is that most of the world neither fears God nor worships Him correctly! God knows our spiritual darkness. He has winked at our ignorance, but this is about to change. He will send the glorious light of the everlasting gospel throughout the world and expel the darkness that Satan has placed around the subject of God's authority and worship. The honest in heart will receive the first angel's message and begin to worship God according to the truth found in the everlasting gospel.

Worship the Creator

How are human beings to worship God? As said earlier, the worship of our Creator has not been left to human design. God clearly explains in the Ten Commandments how He is to be worshiped. Carefully review the first four commandments. They are found in Exodus 20:3-11:

1.   **"You shall have no other gods before [other than] me."**
2.   **"You shall not make for yourself an idol in the form of anything in heaven above or on the earth beneath or in the waters below. You shall not bow down to them or worship them; for I, the Lord your God, am a jealous God, punishing the children for the sin of the fathers to the third and fourth generation of those who hate me, but showing love to thousands who love me and keep my commandments."**
3.   **"You shall not misuse the name of the Lord your God, for the Lord will not hold anyone guiltless who misuses his name."**
4.   **"Remember the Sabbath day by keeping it holy. Six days you shall labor and do all your work, but the seventh day is a Sabbath to the Lord your God. On it you shall not do any work, neither you, nor your son or daughter, nor your manservant or maidservant, nor your animals, nor the alien within your gates. For in six days the Lord made the heavens and the earth, the sea, and all that is in them, but he rested on the seventh day. Therefore the Lord blessed the Sabbath day and made it holy."**

These commandments outline the basics of true worship. They explain the reverence and respect due our Creator. We are not to obey or reverence any other god. We are not to create an idol and bow down before it. We are not to use or represent the name of God in a careless way. And we are to keep the seventh day holy as a memorial to our Creator and His creation of Earth.

The Ten Commandments are divided into two groups. The first four commandments deal with man's relationship to God, and the last six deal with man's relationship to his neighbor. Actually, the Ten Commandments sum up both laws of life. Jesus said, **"...'Love the Lord your God with** all your heart and with all your soul and with all your mind.' This is the first and greatest commandment. And the second is like it: 'Love your neighbor as yourself.' All the Law and the Prophets hang on these two commandments." (Matthew 22:37-40; Jesus quotes from Deuteronomy 6:5; Leviticus 19:18.)

Love is the basis of salvation. Love makes submission a joy. If love is the foundation of a relationship, it is genuine. The two commandments mentioned by Jesus are expanded in the Ten Commandments. The meaning of love is not left to human definition either. In fact, the word "love" today commonly means sex, lust or passion. What a perversion! Jesus came from Heaven to correct human misunderstanding on this point. According to Jesus, true love is a high and holy principle that produces joyful obedience! "Whoever has my commands and obeys them, he is the one who loves me. He who loves me will be loved by my Father, and I too will love him and show myself to him.... If anyone loves me, he will obey my teaching.... He who does not love me will not obey my teaching...." (John 14:21-24)

Satan has veiled the importance of the first four commandments from most of the world. He has specifically hidden the requirements of the fourth commandment which contains divine instruction on the time of worship. Satan's purpose for doing this is quite simple. If people forget their Creator, they will turn to other gods, for man innately needs a god. Man needs something to look up to — something to worship. We were created with this basic need. When man forgets his Creator, he soon creates his own god(s). God asks us to set aside one-seventh of our time for worship and one-tenth of our money for tithe, and most of us, not realizing our accountability to our Creator, give Him neither!

Satan has enjoyed enormous success in displacing the Creator with manmade gods. In fact, everyone gives at least one-seventh of his/her time and one-tenth of his/her money to some god. We only need to discover where the time and money goes to know who or what the god is!

The trumpets will strip away our false sense of security and our foolish attraction for gods of wood, metal and stone, and all people of the world will be awakened to see their rebellious attitude against God. The knowledge of the true, living and omnipotent God will break out all over the Earth!

God's silence will be shattered, and all creation will know that He sits enthroned in Heaven. He is Almighty. The everlasting gospel will contain a clarion call to worship the Creator on His holy day — Saturday, the seventh day of the week.

Review the fourth commandment on page 72 and notice the following:

1. The seventh day of the week was declared holy because God rested on the seventh day to commemorate the creation of the world! The word *holy* simply means "set apart." God made the seventh day uniquely different from the other six at creation! He set the seventh-day apart from the others. (Genesis 2:2,3) This is no different than marriage. When a man and woman are married, they are set apart from all others by vows of fidelity.

2. Knowing that Satan would lead the world to forget or deny the holiness of the seventh-day Sabbath, God begins the fourth commandment with "Remember." (Exodus 20:8)

3. The seventh day alone is holy. The other six days, according to divine law, are for our use and work. (Exodus 20:9)

Were the Ten Commandments abolished?

If you ask most Christians about the Ten Commandments, they will agree that nine of the ten are valid and important. It is morally wrong to steal, kill, commit adultery, curse God or worship idols. In fact, most of the world intellectually agrees with nine of the Ten Commandments and readily acknowledges that they are basic within a moral society. But if you ask about the fourth commandment, you will suddenly hear that the Ten Commandments were nailed to the cross and are no longer binding.

For centuries Protestant and Catholic clerics have taught that the Ten Commandments *are not* binding. Therefore, most laymen see no reason to be concerned about the contents of the fourth commandment. If we reason from cause to effect, we would recognize the hopeless state in which our society finds itself today is due to lawlessness. Parents have not taught their children the importance of law. Where there is no moral law, there is no moral order because where there is no moral law, the law of the jungle prevails. In the jungle, the strongest rule by evil whim. When God's laws are made void, safety, virtue and morality flee. The result is chaos, death, suffering and sexual depravity beyond description. If there is no beacon of moral law within the heart of the human being, there is decadence, chaos and misery. This is the great tragedy of this century. The world now sees the degenerate conduct of millions of youth in the United States whose parents have deprived them knowledge of the basic moral law of life and nobility.

Law and grace

Many Christians refuse to consider the close harmony that exists between law and grace even though they apply these concepts in their lives every day. Law and grace are brother and sister — they are inseparably related. In fact, they cannot exist without each other. We need grace *because* there is law. If God had no law, grace would not be necessary! Paul and John say that when there is no law, there is no sin! (See Romans 4:15 and 1 John 3:4-6.) However, grace does not lessen the obedience required by law either! (Romans 3:31)

If a judge pardons a speeding ticket, does grace release the offender from future obedience to the speed limit? Not at all. The law remains intact, and grace allows the offender another chance. In practice, the harmony between law and grace is easy to understand. For example, when two people are united in love, there are certain non-negotiable rules that must be followed if fidelity to the relationship is to be maintained. Faithfulness is one non-negotiable rule. So it is with our Creator. If we love Him, we must abide by His non-negotiable rules, not for the purpose of salvation, but for the purpose of maintaining a relationship. A person cannot have a relationship with God without obedience to God. He is not our equal. He is Sovereign God of the Universe. The Bible says, **"When Abram was ninety-nine years old, the LORD appeared to him and said, 'I am God Almighty; walk before me and be blameless.'"** (Genesis 17:1) Abram, as well as Enoch and Noah, all walked before God and were blameless, not because of their actions, but because they loved God. (Genesis 5:24; 6:9)

The relationship between God's law and man often confuses the Christian. So understand that obedience to the laws of God has never brought salvation, for *salvation is not based on obedience.* Salvation is based on our "willingness" to obey. Obedience to the laws of God are singularly for our benefit —

not His. This is why disobeying God's laws always brings suffering and death. If we walk according to God's laws, there is fullness of life and everything that God created life to be can be realized. If we walk contrary to God's laws, death and misery are the end results. Corporately speaking, God only pours out His wrath when lawlessness reaches epidemic proportions. The Bible shows that when sin and rebellion fills up the cup, God acts in wrath *for the larger benefit* of succeeding generations.

So, God's non-negotiable rules for man are His Ten Commandments. If we live by them, we can enjoy the pursuit of happiness and the fullness of life that He wants us to have. If we ignore them, the consequences are self-evident. Just watch the evening news.

Categories of people

People may be grouped into a variety of categories concerning the authority of the Ten Commandments.

a. There are people ignorant of the requirements of God's law. These people have not had sufficient reason or opportunity to know and inquire about God's authority or will.

b. There are people who are negligent or careless about God's law. These people know about God's law, but the pursuit of Earthly things causes them to confuse common things with sacred things. Religious matters eventually become a low priority.

c. There are people who observe the law as a ritual necessary for salvation. These people think they keep the law and feel justified by their assumed righteousness. Being technically right on a few points is very important to these people.

d. There are people who deny implicit law. These people reject the idea that the Ten Commandments are necessary or binding today. Most Christians hold this to be true without realizing the awful consequences of what they believe. When pressed on this matter, most Christians will admit that a violation of any of the remaining nine of the Ten Commandments is sin.

e. There are people who openly and defiantly rebel against God's law. These do not want to know God and do not care what He says.

f. There are people seeking to know God and sincerely wanting to live in harmony with the principles of God's law. These are willing to go where God sends, to be all that He wants, and to do all that He asks.

This last group lives by faith. They realize that the law of God is based on two great principles: love to God and love to man. Obeying the first four commandments reveals our love to God, and obeying the last six reveals love to man. Those who obey the commandments of Jesus *out of gratitude and love* know His salvation. They live a life of faith and they are well aware that obedience does not merit or bring salvation.

There is a two-step process to harmonizing our life with the law of God. First, we must realize that we cannot save ourselves through obedience to the law and that inherently, our nature is attracted to sin or lawlessness. This is why we need grace — for all have sinned. Second, those willing to live by faith recognize that Jesus alone can transform our sinful nature. *Victory over sin does not come by human will alone — victory comes through an empowering relationship with Jesus.* By opening our minds and hearts to the sweet influence of the Holy Spirit, we receive power to be overcomers. Our carnal nature is diminished through the power of the Holy Spirit! Sinners become saints through this miraculous process! Jesus said, **"You must be born again,"** (John 3:7) but a person cannot make himself a "born again Christian." Spiritual rebirth occurs when we become willing to obey the commands of Jesus, but this is not the end of the process. We must allow the Holy Spirit to install a new heart within us daily, making us willing to *gobedo* (to go, to be, to do) as God directs. Jesus promised, **"...I will put my laws in their minds and write them on their hearts. I will be their God, and they will be my people."** (Hebrews 8:10) **"You are my friends if you do what I command."** (John 15:14)

A test of faith

God has carefully designed a final exam for Earth. By allowing Satan and his forces to gain complete control of the world's religious and political systems for a short time, God will see who is willing, on pain of severe penalties, to obey His law! He will see who, by faith, would rather die than obey the devil.

Consider this issue carefully. Circumstances will be so desperate during the Great Tribulation that obeying the Ten Commandments will be impossible except by faith! In other words, those who obey Jesus and keep His commandments will only be able to do so through faith in His promises. This is why John identified the remnant as follows, **"Then the dragon was enraged at the woman and went off to make war against the rest of her offspring — those who obey God's commandments and hold to the testimony of Jesus."** (Revelation 12:17)

The third angel speaks loudly

If you have doubts that John was talking about the Ten Commandments when he identified the characteristics of the remnant in the previous text, then look at the third and last warning message to be given to the world. John says, **"A third angel followed them [the first two angels] and said in a loud voice: 'If anyone worships the beast [Satan] and his image and receives his mark on the forehead or on the hand, he, too, will drink of the wine of God's fury, which has been poured full strength into the cup of his wrath. He will be tormented with burning sulfur in the presence of the holy angels and of the Lamb....' This calls for patient endurance on the part of the saints who obey God's commandments and remain faithful to Jesus."** (Revelation 14:9-12)

These verses contain the most solemn warning ever presented to the human race. The coming contest will be simple. It is one of submission! Whom will you obey? God has designed final events so that all can see who has enough faith to obey His Ten Commandments. Is it any wonder that Jesus asked when here on Earth: **"...However, when the Son of Man comes, will He find *faith* on the earth?"** (Luke 18:8)

God personally insures that all inhabitants of earth will hear His third message. It will be powerfully proclaimed by the 144,000 when Satan physically appears on earth. This message is specifically directed at the lamb-like beast that comes up out of the earth and his followers. The devil is called the lamb-like beast because he is the imposter of the Lamb. (Revelation 13:11) The devil will claim to be God! Notice the following points:

1.   If any person obeys (submits to) the laws of the devil (the lamb-like beast), he will be tormented with burning sulfur in the presence of the Lamb of God!
2.   If anyone chooses to receive the tattoo (the mark) of the devil on their right hand or forehead — which will be required to buy or sell — he or she will receive God's wrath full strength!
3.   Those people refusing to worship according to the dictates of the devil must be patient in their suffering. Many people will be killed because they refuse to submit to the devil. They are identified by John as obeying God's commandments and remaining faithful to Jesus. (See Revelation 12:17, 14:12.)

It has been shown that one of the Ten Commandments specifically deals with God's day of worship. Satan knows this, and for this reason, he has obscured the importance of the fourth commandment and led the world into worshiping on days other than the Lord's day. According to the Bible, the Lord's day is *Saturday*, the seventh day of the week. Jesus said, **"...the Son of Man is Lord even of the Sabbath."** (Mark 2:28) Many Christians mistakenly think that Sunday is the Lord's day even though the Bible never suggests that the first day of the week is the Lord's day.

Reasons to worship on Sunday?

There is no command for Sunday worship in all the Bible. When governments make and enforce laws regarding the sacredness of a day of worship to appease God, they will quickly go from national apostasy to national ruin. For example, shortly after the first four trumpets, the United States will implement regulations regarding the sacredness of Sunday, but Sunday *is not*, nor has it ever been, God's day of worship. Sunday laws will openly defy the law of Almighty God, specifically the fourth commandment!

Many God fearing people mistakenly believe that Sunday is the Lord's day. Scholars have produced a number of glossy *reasons* to confirm the error. But, what is the confused reasoning of a scholar compared to the authority of God — even a direct order from the Almighty?

Watch for this: When the Sunday laws are implemented, clerics will use selected texts from the Bible to assure millions that already worship on Sunday that God wants man to worship on Sunday. Because most Americans already believe that Sunday is the Lord's day, this will not seem inappropriate to the *majority*. Since there are only eight texts in the New Testament that mention the first day of the week, Biblical support for the sacredness of Sunday will have to come exclusively from *these* verses. Here are the texts:

Matthew 28:1
Mark 16:2
Mark 16:9
Luke 24:1
John 20:1
John 20:19
Acts 20:7
1 Corinthians 16:2

The first six texts refer to the resurrection of Jesus on the first day of the week — a well known fact. However, none of these texts say anything about the *sacredness* of Sunday. In fact, Luke 23:56 points out that a group of women did not prepare His body for burial on Friday, but rested on the Sabbath "according to the commandment." The point here is that Jesus had not informed His followers that the fourth commandment was going to be made void because of His death.

Since the first six texts simply discuss the resurrection of Jesus, we'll investigate the remaining two verses and note the absence of any command from God for the observance of Sunday.

Acts 20:7

Some preachers refer to Acts 20 for evidence that Sunday worship was practiced by the apostles. Notice, **"On the first day of the week we came together to break bread. Paul spoke to the people and, because he intended to leave the next day, kept on talking until midnight."** (Acts 20:7) Now, consider the details within this verse.

In Bible times, a day began at sunset and ended the following evening. Since creation, the rotation of the earth has produced this unchanging process. (See Genesis 1.) The Jews in Christ's time regarded a day from evening to evening and kept the Sabbath from Friday sundown to Saturday sundown. Compare Luke 23:50-56 with Leviticus 23:32.

So, the timing described in Acts 20:7 is as follows: Paul stayed with the believers at Troas for seven days. (Acts 20:6) At the evening of the first day of the week, at supper time, the believers came together to eat supper with Paul and to say good-bye to their friend. The first day of the week in Paul's time began Sabbath evening at sundown, or what we now call Saturday evening. After supper, Paul preached until midnight, or Saturday midnight. A few hours later on Sunday morning, the first day of the week, he left Troas for Assos.

So, Paul met with believers for supper and preached until midnight, Saturday night. Does a farewell supper and Saturday night meeting change or abrogate the fourth commandment of God? No. Even if Paul chose to worship on Tuesday night, would this make void the law of God? No. Only God can make void His law.

Some preachers claim that the term "breaking of bread" indicates Paul's visit was a communion or worship service. Not so. In Luke 24:13-31 Jesus "broke bread" at supper time with His disciples after walking more than seven miles to Emmaus with them. The breaking of bread, even to this day, remains a custom in the Orient because bread is often baked so firm that it has to be literally broken in order to eat it. We know that Jesus "broke bread" on Thursday night with His disciples at Passover, so why would Jesus conduct worship service at sundown in Emmaus, as the second day of the week was beginning? Even if it was a worship service, where is God's command making void His fourth commandment? Is it in Acts 20:7? No.

I call Acts 20:7 a mystery text because Paul did not conduct a Sunday service in Troas. Actually, he held a meeting on Saturday night — the first part of the first day of the week in Bible times — but is now reckoned as the last part of the seventh day. (Jews reckon a day from sundown to sundown. Today, we reckon a day from midnight to midnight.) So, if Christians really took Paul's example for authority on the time of worship, they would worship on Saturday night (sundown to midnight). So, where is the authority in this text for Sunday observance?

1 Corinthians 16:2

Some Christians argue Paul insists that offerings for the poor be taken on the first day of the week. Notice: **"Now about the collection for God's people: Do what I told the Galatian churches to do. On the first day of every week, each one of you should set aside a sum of money in keeping with his income, saving it up, so that when I come no collections will have to be made. Then, when I arrive, I will give letters of introduction to the men you approve and send them with your gift to Jerusalem."** (1 Corinthians 16:1-3)

In Paul's day, money was not a common medium of exchange like it is today. Most trading was done with barter; that is, a person might trade a chicken or something for cloth or pottery. Paul instructed the church in Corinth to begin each week with selling or trading so they might obtain a sum of currency. He wanted to take *money* with him to give to the persecuted believers in Jerusalem. Since Paul would not be able to travel with roosters, goats, pottery and other things of value, he asked that they take care of this matter, "first thing after the Sabbath." (Compare with Nehemiah 13:15.) Again, the question is asked, "Does Paul's instruction change or make void the fourth commandment of God?" Not at all.

Thoughts on Romans 6

Some Christians suggest that worship on Sunday is proper because Jesus arose from the dead on Sunday morning, the first day of the week. Yes, the resurrection is important, and the Bible does provide a celebration of the resurrection! It is called *baptism*. Notice what Paul says, **"What shall we say, then? Shall we go on sinning so that grace may increase? By no means! We died to sin; how can we live in it any longer? Or don't you know that all of us who were baptized into Christ Jesus were baptized into his death? We were therefore buried with him through baptism into death in order that, just as Christ was raised**

from the dead through the glory of the Father, we too may live a new life." (Romans 6:1-4)

Does baptism change or abrogate the fourth commandment? Not at all. In fact, not one of the eight texts in the New Testament says that the holiness of the seventh day was ever transferred to Sunday!

What was nailed to the cross?

Many Christians argue that the Ten Commandments were nailed to the cross. Yet, this argument does not solve the problem. Whatever happens to the fourth commandment, happens to the other nine! If we do away with the fourth commandment that declares the seventh day to be a holy day, we must also do away with the commandment that says adultery is wrong. Paul wrote, **"What shall we say, then? Is the law sin? Certainly not! Indeed I would not have known what sin was except through the law. For I would not have known what coveting really was if the law had not said, 'Do not covet.' "** (Romans 7:7)

So, what was nailed to the cross? Only the ceremonies of the sanctuary services that were a shadow or explanation of the plan of salvation were nailed to the cross. The key word here is *shadow*. Notice what Paul said, **"For in Christ all the fullness of the Deity lives in bodily form, and you have been given fullness in Christ, who is the head over every power and authority.... When you were dead in your sins and in the uncircumcision of your sinful nature, God made you alive with Christ. He forgave us all our sins, having canceled the written code, with its regulations, that was against us and that stood opposed to us; he took it away, nailing it to the cross.... Therefore do not let anyone judge you by what you eat or drink, or with regard to a religious festival, a New Moon celebration or a Sabbath day. These are a shadow of the things that were to come; the reality, however, is found in Christ. Do not let anyone who delights in false humility and the worship of angels disqualify you for the prize...."** (Colossians 2:9-18)

If you'll look at these verses carefully, you'll see that Paul is talking about the regulations regarding *religious feasts, New Moon observances and Sabbath days*. The Sabbath days that Paul is talking about is not *the* Sabbath day of the fourth commandment. Rather, the term Sabbath days here applies to Sabbath "feast days" such as the Passover or the Day of Atonement. (Leviticus 16:31) Certain feast days fell on different days of the week (like our birthday) because they occurred on the same date each year. These feast days were special Sabbaths of rest that pointed forward to different aspects of the death and ministry of Jesus. For example, the Passover not only reminded the Jews of deliverance from Egypt, it pointed forward to the time when the Passover Lamb — Jesus Christ — would die so that all could be delivered from the bondage of sin!

The Jews confused the Ten Commandment law of God with the laws of Moses, much like we do today. Even though one set of laws was written by the finger of God on two tablets of stone, and the other by the hand of a man, the Jews did not understand the relationship between the moral law written by the finger of God and the ceremonial laws written by the hand of Moses. One law was permanent, the other was temporary. The greater law written by God Himself was kept inside the ark. This is why the ark was often called the ark of the covenant. (The Ten Commandments are the basis of God's covenant with man. This covenant says, **"If you choose to obey me, I will be your God."** Deuteronomy 30:9-11) The lesser law of Moses, containing ceremonial rules, was kept in a pocket on the side of the ark. (See Deuteronomy 10:1,2; 31:26.)

Other objections

What about Romans 14? Some Christians use Romans to prove it does not matter which day of the week we use to worship God. Notice the text: **"Accept him whose faith is weak, without passing judgment on disputable matters. One man's faith allows him to eat everything, but another man, whose faith is weak, eats only vegetables. The man who eats everything must not look down on him who does not, and the man who does not eat everything must not condemn the man who does, for God has accepted him. Who are you to judge someone else's servant? To his own master he stands or falls. And he will stand, for the Lord is able to make him stand. One man considers one day more sacred than another; another man considers every day alike. Each one should be fully convinced in his own mind. He who regards one day as special,** does so to the Lord. He who eats meat, eats to the Lord, for he gives thanks to God; and he who abstains, does so to the Lord and gives thanks to God. For none of us lives to himself alone and none of us dies to himself alone. If we live, we live to the Lord; and if we die, we die to the Lord. So, whether we live or die, we belong to the Lord. For this very reason, Christ died and returned to life so that he might be the Lord of both the dead and the living. You, then, why do you judge your brother? Or why do you look down on your brother? For we will all stand before God's judgment seat." (Romans 14:1-10)

The context of these verses does not imply that we can worship God whenever we feel like it. No, this text is addressing a specific problem that early Christians had to deal with; namely, the religious customs of the Jews. In other words, if a new believer in Jesus felt he needed to observe Passover, Paul did not condemn the new believer except to say that his faith was weak. Also, if the new believer could not consciously eat meat purchased in the market place for fear it had not been killed correctly or that it had been offered before idols, Paul said, leave him alone! (The Jews would not purchase nor eat meat unless it was killed according to Mosaic code. Leviticus 19:26) Today, many clerics use this text as support for Sunday worship, although I seriously doubt they will use it when they seek the exaltation of Sunday through the enforcement of law. Some Christians say that Pentecost came on Sunday the year that Christ died, therefore, Sunday is God's holy day. The fact is, Pentecost has always fallen on Sunday — ever since the Exodus. The Wavesheaf offering was made on the first Sunday after Passover and Pentecost, 50 days (counting inclusively) occurred on Sunday. (Leviticus 23). So, the annual Pentecost feast took place on Sunday for more than a millennium before Jesus came to Earth. Does this make the fourth commandment void? No.

Last, some clerics claim that nine of the Ten Commandments are mentioned in the New Testament, but the fourth commandment is missing. Does the absence of the fourth commandment prove it is void or does its absence affirm the assumption of New Testament writers that the Sabbath remains intact without question? Paul clears this up *in the New Testament* by saying, **"There remains, then, a Sabbath-rest for the people of God; for anyone who enters God's rest also rests from his own work, just as God did from his."** (Hebrews 4:9,10)

Which is the greatest law?

As you might expect of a legalistic society, the Jews loved to argue about their laws. An expert lawyer even challenged Jesus with a test to see which law was the greatest! (Matthew 22:34-40) I believe the spirituality of the Jews degenerated into a great legal system of darkness, because they generally misunderstood the purpose of God's laws. (Matthew 23:2-15)

When the apostle Paul began to explain the purposes and relationships between the ceremonial laws and God's moral law, you can understand the Jewish hatred exercised against him. Paul claimed that the laws of Moses had expired, and this was more than the Jews could tolerate! Paul was captured and eventually beheaded for his convictions. (Acts 21:27-36)

Paul is very explicit in Colossians 2. He points out that the laws nailed to the cross were laws regarding the *shadows* of the real thing. The ceremonial laws requiring the observance of new moons, Sabbath feasts and the sacrifice of lambs became unnecessary because the Lamb of God had died and the shadow of salvation was now open to full view. In other words, ceremonial laws were temporary until their meaning was fulfilled. Moral laws are not temporary, because love never ends. One law was written on paper; the other on stone. One law was penned by man; the other, by God. Doesn't this say something about their enduring nature?

So, consider Paul's dilemma. How could he get the Jews to understand the meaning of the laws and cease doing something they had been doing for nearly 1,800 years? We have the same problem today. How can a whole nation change from Sunday observance to Saturday observance?

Paul is very clear in Hebrews 10 and Galatians 3 & 4 that ceremonies never brought salvation to the Jews in the first place; rather, they were temporary and were designed to teach *how* salvation occurs! Paul is also clear that obeying the Ten Commandments cannot produce salvation, because salvation only comes by faith! The problem today is that most Christians think that faith and grace makes the law unnecessary. Does love between husband and wife eliminate the necessity for fidelity? No. Neither does living together make two persons married. The relationship between love and obedience is simple. God grants salvation to everyone who becomes willing to do His will. He does not grant salvation to us on our ability to do His will. We demonstrate our willingness by receiving strength from

God to do what He wants. Paul understood this process. (See Romans 7.) In fact, all through his life, Paul faithfully observed the seventh-day Sabbath. (See Acts 13:44; 16:13; 17:2; 18:4,11.) Even more, Jesus pointed out that the seventh-day Sabbath would remain sacred years after His ascension! (Matthew 24:20)

Can't break one commandment

If we take the position that Jesus nailed the fourth commandment to the cross, then we must conclude that He also nailed nine others, too. Whatever we do with the fourth commandment, we must also do with the other nine. This issue will become the all important distinction between those loving God and those rebelling against Him. The Ten Commandments are non-negotiable. They stand as a unit representing the revealed will of God. The Ten Commandments were written on two tables of stone because they are based on two enduring principles: love to God and love to man. The first four commandments explain how we are to love God. The last six commandments explain how we are to love our neighbor. One more point: Maturity in Christ begins when we acknowledge the binding claims of God's law, and realizing our great weaknesses, we place our faith in Jesus so that we can fulfill His law through His indwelling power.

Paul knew that all Ten Commandments were intact. He said, **"For I would not have known what it was to covet if the law had not said, 'Do not covet.' "** (Romans 7:7)

James wrote, **"If you really keep the royal law found in Scripture, 'Love your neighbor as yourself,' you are doing right! But if you show favoritism, you sin and are convicted by the law as lawbreakers. For whoever keeps the whole law and yet stumbles at just one point is guilty of breaking all of it. For he who said, 'Do not commit adultery,' also said, 'Do not murder.' If you do not commit adultery but do commit murder, you have become a lawbreaker."** (James 2:8-11)

James brings us to an important and fundamental conclusion regarding the royal law, the King's law. He says we must obey *all* the commandments. If we break one, we're guilty of breaking them all, because the King's law is only fulfilled by love. We must first love God with all our heart, mind and soul and then our neighbor as ourselves. How should our love for God be expressed? Jesus said, **"If you love me, you will obey what I command."** (John 14:15)

Keeping the Sabbath holy will not save anyone. Mandating Saturday laws will not save anyone either! This is why the final exam of the human race is carefully designed *to test our relationship* with Jesus: The basis of salvation is faith. Faith is doing what God requires at any cost. Since eternal life only comes by faith, and since every means of human survival will be cut off, you and I will have to have great faith in order to *obey* God! If it is hard now, what will it be then?

Unholy war?

So, consider this. The devil will lead the world to openly rebel against God's truth. I believe he will eventually unite the world in worship on Sunday because 1.5 billion Catholics and Protestants already worship on this day. (These two groups will form the largest constituency within Babylon.) Stringent laws will be made to ensure that all people worship as the devil dictates. (Revelation 13:15,16) Thus, the devil will set himself up before the world as the living God. He will receive the worship due God and exult in his deceptive tricks. Paul says, **"He (Satan) opposes and exalts himself over everything that is called God or is worshiped, and even sets himself up in God's temple, proclaiming himself to be God."** (2 Thessalonians 2:4) This prediction will be fulfilled soon after the fifth trumpet sounds.

The sixth trumpet

This trumpet will be a global war which Satan initiates to force all nations into agreement on a one-world government. God allows Satan the power to conduct this war at just the right time. Notice what John says, **"The sixth angel blew his trumpet... and the four angels (bound at the great river Euphrates) who had been kept ready for this very hour and day and month and year were released to kill a third of mankind. The number of mounted troops was two hundred million. I heard their number.... A third of mankind was killed by the three plagues of fire,** smoke and sulfur that came out of their mouths. The rest of mankind that were not killed by these plagues still did not repent of the work of their hands... nor of their murders, their magic arts, their sexual immorality or their thefts." (Revelation 9:13-21)

What Satan cannot achieve through deceit, he accomplishes through force. This is always the last resort of false religion. The sixth trumpet war will involve all nations of the world. The followers of Satan within each nation will be directed by Satan to take control of their respective nations. Those opposed to the heavy demands of the devil will resist, although they also refuse to worship God. The result is that the world will be in a global civil war with itself! Americans will be fighting Americans. Africans will fight Africans. Europeans will fight one another, etc.

The angels of God will hold back the tide of Satan's advance until the gospel has reached almost every person. Then, this war will accomplish two things. First, warfare will force everyone to finally choose which "Lamb" they will obey — the one on earth claiming to be God, or the Lamb who will soon come in the clouds of glory. Second, the war will reveal who the remnant are! They will clearly stand out from the rest of the world.

Antichrist reigns as God

By the end of the sixth trumpet war, everyone will have made their decision. Many will obey and worship the devil for the sake of survival even though they know it is wrong. They will choose the mark of the beast rather than live by faith. Understand this point: If our obedience is not based on faith in Jesus, one cannot stand the test of truth. In the future, millions will compromise their religious beliefs; they will receive the mark or permit of the beast so that they can buy food and conduct business. John says, **"The rest of mankind that was not killed (in the war) did not repent of their (evils)."** (Revelation 9:20)

Those receiving the mark of the beast will be committed to open rebellion against the law of God. Since everyone on earth has already made their decision and nothing more can be done to save humanity, the door to salvation closes in Heaven. Jesus then concludes His mediatorial ministry on behalf of the people of Earth. The seventh trumpet sounds; it is an

announcement that salvation has ended and that time has come for the
outpouring of the seven last plagues. An earthquake, greater than the one
marking the beginning of the trumpets, will occur. This and spectacular
scenes in the heavens will announce that the plan of salvation is finished.

Only the faith–full will survive

Only those willing to live by faith will endure. Millions will die for their
faith, others will survive — but only by faith. John is very clear that
Babylon's forces will kill a large number of God's people. But understand
that when the seventh trumpet sounds, martyrdom ends because God delivers
His people from death. (Daniel 12:1) Can you, like Job, say, **"Though He
slay me, yet I will hope in Him"**? (Job 13:15) A real testing time is just
before us. The test is *faith*. Will you stand firm even if everyone in your
family is joining the ranks of the enemy?

What about today?

I am often asked how one reconciles the nearness of these events with
decisions about life that must be made today. For example, what does a
person do about plans for college, marriage, building or buying a new
home, the expansion of business, retirement savings, career requirements,
etc? I have found one answer for all these questions. It is this: Earnestly
seek God for wisdom. He has promised to direct you. As you patiently
seek Him, God will show you just what He wants. (Proverbs 3:5) So, learn
now to live by faith. Put your whole confidence in God. The ultimate test
of having a relationship with Jesus is being able to hear His voice. Jesus
said, **"My sheep listen to my voice; I know them, and they follow me."**
(John 10:27)

Chapter 6

A dramatic rescue by Jesus

This book draws to an end with a review and an invitation. A review of the eternal gospel is necessary because the gospel sets before us an all-or-nothing proposition. In due time, we will either accept or reject the gospel of Jesus because of the basic human need to resolve conflicts. Some people try to avoid difficult decisions by putting them far into the background of consciousness. They say, "I will think about this tomorrow." Postponement, though, is really a decision, too. Suppose you asked your sweetheart to marry you right away. Any answer other than "yes" is actually a "no," isn't it? The danger with postponement is that it "candy coats" our rejection until we are trapped by our own inaction. In the case of the gospel, we must listen to the Holy Spirit today. We must be "born again" and we cannot accomplish this on our own. Only through the ministry of the Holy Spirit will we obtain the desire to change our carnal nature. Therefore, it is important to remember that there is a limit to the Holy Spirit's promptings — He will not work with us forever. (Hebrews 3:7-15)

If the Holy Spirit has impressed you that this message is important, you need to restudy it carefully for two reasons. First, your understanding will increase 100% the second time you go through it. Details will become much clearer and more meaningful. Second, now that you understand the contents of Revelation, you need to find an interested friend and share this message. **"The Spirit and the bride say, 'Come!' And let him who hears say, 'Come!' Whoever is thirsty, let him come; and whoever wishes, let him take the free gift of the water of life."** (Revelation 22:17)

The proclamation of the gospel

The full gospel must reach every person before Jesus comes. John said, **"Then I saw another angel flying in midair, and he had the eternal gospel to proclaim to those who live on the earth — to every nation, tribe, language and people."** (Revelation 14:6) Jesus said, **"And this gospel of the kingdom will be preached in the whole world as a testimony to all nations, and then the end will come."** (Matthew 24:14) The question is, "What is the gospel, and who will help spread it?"

What is the gospel?

In two sentences, the eternal gospel is this: All of us have sinned; therefore, we are condemned by God's law to death — but Jesus took our place and paid the price for our sins. If we put our faith in Jesus and surrender to His commandments, we will be saved. Look at salvation from God's perspective. Many people honestly live up to all they know to be right, and Jesus understands this. In His great mercy, He accepts those people who are sincere in heart and do not know or understand the great truths of the gospel. *Jesus does not hold a person responsible for truth he does not know or cannot know.* On the contrary, James tells us that sin is held against us when we know better and then refuse to do it! **"Anyone, then, who knows the good he ought to do and doesn't do it, sins."** (James 4:17) The Lord loves the people of earth with a love beyond human understanding. Those living up to all they know to be right glorify God and He is pleased with them. Peter says, **"For the eyes of the Lord are on the righteous and his ears are attentive to their prayer, but the face of the Lord is against those who do evil."** (1 Peter 3:12) Because God's truth has been obscured from most of the world by Satan's devices, Jesus will soon awaken the world to hear the gospel. Those people who are sincere in heart will rejoice to learn more and they will embrace the truth as it continues to unfold in revealing the eternal gospel. Thus, the remnant will be gathered out of all religious systems into one body under the leadership of Jesus. Jesus said, **"I have other sheep that are not of this sheep pen. I must bring them also. They too will listen to my voice, and there shall be one flock and one shepherd."** (John 10:16)

So, the net effect of the gospel in the last days will be to unify those who hear the voice of Jesus into one last group called the remnant. This will be accomplished during the time-period of the trumpets by separating sheep from goats. People will either receive the gospel and by faith, obey the commandments of Jesus as the three angel's messages command, or they will reject the gospel and eventually choose the mark of the beast. There will be no middle ground. The rapid sequence of events, coupled with rigorous laws requiring disobedience to the law of God will push everyone into a rapid decision.

What must I do to be saved?

One of Satan's most powerful deceptions has two sides. The devil has led many to believe that salvation either comes through obedience to God or by intellectual assent to what is true. Satan's trickery is very subtle. He can actually make evil people think they are righteous! For example, Satan led the Pharisees to think they were righteous even though they were far away from the kingdom. Jesus said to them, **"...on the outside you appear to people as righteous but on the inside you are full of hypocrisy and wickedness."** (Matthew 23:28)

The Pharisees believed they were righteous. From their point of view, they could see nothing wrong with themselves. So, how can a person know if his life is acceptable to God? Jesus said, **"...every good tree bears good fruit, a good tree cannot bear bad fruit, but a bad tree bears bad fruit, and a bad tree cannot bear good fruit."** (Matthew 7:17,18) Religious people often say one thing and do another. So, we must test ourselves from time to time to see if we are in Christ! Paul wrote, **"Examine yourselves to see whether you are in the faith; test yourselves. Do you not realize that Christ Jesus is in you--unless, of course, you fail the test?"** (2 Corinthians 13:5)

How do we test ourselves? Perhaps we can look at two extreme examples to see if Jesus is really in our hearts. The first example describes a religious type of people called "workers." These individuals are *working* their way to Heaven but do not know it. The second group of people are called "thinkers." This group *thinks* they have salvation because they agree with the Bible.

The workers

"Workers" say, "I am saved by faith," even though they are actually working their way to Heaven. People who have this characteristic are usually identified by zealous and/or rigorous obedience to the teachings or ideals of their denomination. Workers tend to see sin as acts of *commission*, that is, sins or wrongful deeds acted out. To live within the rules is very important to these people. In their hearts, they have confidence that they are saved because they are obedient to all the rules. They look at themselves and see very little wrong. Workers, in day to day living, regard obedience as the *primary process* through which salvation occurs, even though they may say, "Salvation comes by faith!"

The Jewish religion at the time of Christ typifies this great deception. The major sin that blinds these people is pride. They cannot see why they should not have salvation! After all, they do not see anything wrong with themselves! These people criticize the "outsiders" who break the rules but they rarely speak about their own sins of *omission*. Jesus said to the Pharisees, **"Woe to you Pharisees, because you give God a tenth of your mint, rue and all other kinds of garden herbs, but you neglect justice and the love of God. You should have practiced the latter without leaving the former undone. ...And you experts in the law, woe to you, because you load people down with burdens they can hardly carry, and you yourselves will not lift one finger to help them."** (Luke 11:42,46)

The coming tribulation will overtake the workers. Workers will not be able to obey God in the days ahead, for civil laws will become so strict and the penalty so great that obedience will be impossible! (Remember how Hitler threatened the German people — if anyone helped a Jew, that person would be punished just as the Jews were.) To avoid suffering and the possibility of death, workers will have no option but to submit to the laws of Babylon! When the great religious organizations of the world merge as a result of the massive destruction by the seven trumpets, whose rules will the workers follow? Without strong faith in God, no one can withstand Babylon.

The tragedy of the worker deception is that the devil makes obedience the object of religion, not the means of having a relationship with Jesus. Jesus said of the Jews, **"They worship me in vain; their teachings are but** rules taught by men. You have let go of the commands of God and are holding on to the traditions of men." (Mark 7:7,8)

The thinkers

On the other end of the scale, Satan has a counterfeit about salvation that is equally dangerous and perhaps more widely received than the worker concept. In brief, this counterfeit maintains that if you *believe* you're saved, you're saved! In general terms, this doctrine teaches that obedience to the Ten Commandments is unnecessary; even more, obedience to the fourth commandment is an insult to God's grace. The Christian is under grace, not under the law, as though grace makes the law null and void. The primary elements of this religion are to say the words: "Jesus is Lord," and to profess love for one's neighbors.

By agreeing with the fact that Jesus died on Calvary, many believe that they have salvation, full and free! But how can our agreement with historical fact bring salvation? James wrote, **"You believe that there is one God. Good! Even the demons believe that — and shudder."** (James 2:19)

I call these people "thinkers" because they *think* they receive salvation by some mental process. Thinkers tend to enjoy their religion more than workers because their religion is people-oriented. Workers tend to be more critical of behavior, whereas thinkers are generous and quite casual about behavior. Thinkers claim, God's stringent rules, the Ten Commandments, were done away with at the cross; therefore, anything socially acceptable is acceptable to God. "He accepts us as we are," they claim. So, the thinker's gospel has few requirements. Thinkers conclude that righteousness comes with intellectual assent, so just believe you are saved, and join a church. The heart of the thinker's gospel is the golden rule, "Do unto your neighbor as you would have him do to you."

The thinker's gospel, like the worker's gospel, has some good points. But, both fall short of the target. The essence of religion is to first love God with heart, mind and soul, and your neighbor as yourself. But what is love for God? James asked the same question, **"What good is it, my brothers, if a man claims to have faith but has no deeds? Can such faith save him? Suppose a brother or sister is without clothes and daily food. If** one of you says to him, 'Go, I wish you well; keep warm and well fed,' but does nothing about his physical needs, what good is it? In the same way, faith by itself, if it is not accompanied by action, is dead. But someone will say, 'You have faith; I have deeds.' Show me your faith without deeds, and I will show you my faith by what I do. ... You see that a person is justified by what he does and not by faith alone." (James 2:14-24)

Synthesis

Certain characteristics of thinkers and workers have been presented in the extreme to demonstrate the kinds of behavior that such theological processes produce. What we *do* reveals what we really *believe*!

Satan has cleverly counterfeited the gospel of the workers and thinkers by using *partial* truth in each case! So, do not be fooled. Both doctrines are deadly. The simple truth about salvation is this: Salvation by faith means a complete surrender of the will to Jesus. It means to be all that God asks, do all that God requires, and to go wherever Jesus directs. True salvation produces a life of action. Obedience comes as a result of experiencing salvation — not salvation as a result of obedience. Look closely at Hebrews 11 and you will observe that each of the men and women in this Hall of Faith was obedient to God's commands! Paul says of Abraham, **"By faith Abraham, when God tested him, offered Isaac as a sacrifice. He who had received the promises was about to sacrifice his one and only son, even though God had said to him, 'It is through Isaac that your offspring will be reckoned.' Abraham reasoned that God could raise the dead, and figuratively speaking, he did receive Isaac back from death."** (Hebrews 11:17-19) That old gospel favorite by James Sammis and Daniel Towner, "Trust and Obey," summarizes the gospel message very well:

"When we walk with the Lord
In the light of His Word,
What a glory He sheds on our way!
While we do His good will,
He abides with us still,
And with all who will trust and obey.

> Trust and obey,
> For there's no other way
> To be happy in Jesus,
> But to trust and obey."

Sound asleep?

Many Christians scoff at the suggestion that the Lord will return this decade. They see no reason for all the excitement. They say, "All things continue as usual — why all the fuss?" These people are content in their spiritual poverty. They have no idea about the events coming upon the earth, and even worse, they do not want to hear about it! They like religious programming — entertainment that features talented singers and gifted speakers with clever ideas. They do not want to hear about the wrath of God, or the cross that we must bear. Thus, Satan has convinced many within the Christian church that they are either safe from the tribulation, or that life will continue as usual until Jesus returns. Unfortunately, these deceptions are widely accepted.

Those who understand the everlasting gospel are not focused on gloom or doom. These people are focused on the greatest and most awesome event in earth's history, the revelation of Jesus at the second coming. They know that a testing time, a purifying time, precedes the second coming. They know about the future rise of Babylon and the appearing of Satan claiming to be God. These people know about the "unholy war" that will be waged against them. They know that their faith will be fully tested. Yet, they are positive about their relationship with Jesus, which gives them peace in their hearts. These people are daily claiming the promises of God. They are committed to being "overcomers" because they "have ears to hear what the Spirit is saying to them." They walk by faith and they will be prepared for a mighty work when the trumpets sound.

Worship God

Satan has led most of the world to deny the importance of God's seventh-day Sabbath. Friday is the day of worship for more than one billion Moslems. About 25 million Jews recognize Saturday as God's holy day (but Sabbath without Jesus is like cake with no icing), and one and a half billion Christians (all Christians combined: Catholics, Protestants, Greek Orthodox, Anglican, etc.) believe in the sacredness of Sunday. Nearly three billion people have no regard for the sacredness of any special day of the week.

It should be clear that worshiping on God's holy day does not, nor can it ever, bring salvation to a person. For example, if an alien sneaks into a country and keeps all of the laws, he does not become a citizen by obeying the laws. Rather, an alien becomes a citizen by *submitting* to an immigration process. Part of the process involves taking an oath of allegiance to the laws of that nation. Salvation, in a similar way, comes when we submit our lives to Jesus. This means that we are willing to go, to be and to do as He directs. We put our will aside and place Jesus on the throne of the heart. Then, Jesus directs us. Faith involves obedience to all Ten Commandments. Thus, John identified the remnant as those people having the faith of Jesus; otherwise, they could not obey the commandments of God.

The most wonderful part of God's salvation during the end-time is this: During the Great Tribulation, God is going to give every faith-full person the greatest gift possible. This gift is a completely new nature. It is a nature that loves to render obedience to God — a nature free of rebellion — a nature that is naturally opposed to sin. In short, Jesus is going to bestow His righteous nature on those who want it. (Hebrews 8:10,11)

Get prepared

If the Bible teaches anything, it teaches that salvation comes by faith in Jesus. God knows our fears are great. God knows we have no strength, glory or righteousness. God knows that man is made of the dust of the ground, but God loves us so much that He gave His only Son to die in our place. Yes, the events before us will be frightening and overwhelming. Yes, the coming tribulation will be greater than anything the world has ever known. But, the presence of God will never be closer and His peace more valuable. So, give yourself to Him right now. Tell the Lord that you are willing to be, to do and to go as He commands, and when He comes, YOU will be saved. Jesus guarantees it.

Appendix

Why 1994 appears to be important

Jubilee year 1994 (March 20, 1994 to March 19, 1995) appears to be ominous for four Biblical reasons. Notice that I said, "Biblical reasons." My assertion is independent of the rapid-fire changes in world conditions or global efforts for peace. In fact, I find the process of interpreting the Bible through newspaper headlines to be a faulty approach. Rather, a correct interpretation of Bible prophecy should produce what newspapers will eventually proclaim. As in the days of Noah, God reveals those things about our future that are indispensable to the survival of those who love Him.

Jubilee year 1994 (throughout this book called 1994) appears prophetically significant to me because four distinct themes within the Bible *appear* to intersect near or within that year. In other words, 1994 surfaces as an interesting solution to four Bible themes. No specific scripture says that 1994 is important. However, we must remember that the Scriptures do not implicitly say that 4 B.C., A.D. 27 or A.D. 30 were important either. (Jesus was born in 4 B.C., was baptized in A.D. 27, and died and ascended to Heaven in A.D. 30.)

No time-setting

I do not anticipate the appearing of Jesus in 1994. Neither do I know the date our Lord will return. I am not time-setting. There is an important distinction between time-study and time-setting, and many sincere people confuse the difference. The basic difference between time-setting and time-study is this: Time-setting makes prophetic interpretation time-dependent. On the other hand, time-study does not require that the fulfillment of a prophecy be time-dependent. This point may be illustrated in the following manner. If someone sets a date for the rapture, second coming or whatever and it does not come to pass, the net effect is a complete loss of confidence in the message and its messenger. The net effect is damaging. It is better to say nothing than to set time.

On the other hand, if a certain *time frame* appears to be important within some prophetic context and it does not come to pass, any delay requires a careful re-evaluation of the matter. Notice what Peter said about time-study: **"Concerning this salvation, the prophets, who spoke of the grace that was to come to you, searched intently and with the greatest care, *trying to find out the time* and circumstances to which the Spirit of Christ in them was pointing when he predicted the sufferings of Christ and the glories that would follow."** (1 Peter 1:10,11; emphasis mine)

In the case of time-study, the time frame, the event, or both can be misinterpreted. There are a few time-dependent prophecies in the Bible, but 1994 is not involved in any time-dependent prophecy that I know of. The suggestion that 1994 may be an important year is not time-setting. *My point is that most Bible prophecies are not time-dependent and they should not be so represented.*

Given the superficial interest in prophecy that most people have, the mention of any time frame can be harmful. Many will pick up on a date to test the expositor and his conclusions even if it is only a "suggested" range. For this reason, I have received a lot of scolding for even mentioning 1994. Nevertheless, it is my estimate that the Great Tribulation will begin in 1994 or 1995.

Then, why mention a time frame at all? Aside from Biblical reasons, I also find four personal reasons to mention 1994. First, I've been impressed for several years that the 1990's could be earth's last decade. Second, Christians have cried "Wolf-wolf" for so long that the phrase, "The Lord is coming soon," means nothing. Third, I'm convinced that the appearing of the 144,000 will signal the arrival of the final generation and when they appear, the four winds of Revelation 7 will soon begin to blow. Finally, few human beings get prepared for anything until the time actually arrives.

I know that the mention of a date for any prophetic fulfillment turns some, even many people off. Whether a person is turned on or off about these things is a matter beyond my responsibility. Besides, what does our belief or denial have to do with coming events? My calling is to share the things I have discovered.

Again I say, my understanding of coming events is not time-dependent. The future events predicted in Revelation will surely occur. *When* they will occur remains a matter of study. If or when we see some of the preliminary fulfillments (such as the global earthquake of Revelation 8:2-5), we will surely know that Jesus has begun the irreversible processes predicted in Daniel and Revelation.

A change of mind

In the late 1980's, I calculated the ominous year to be Jubilee year 1992 instead of 1994. However in March of 1991, an error was found in my calculations. I published a correction in our monthly newsletter *Day Star* and subsequently focused my interest on 1994. This change in my understanding demonstrates a crucial difference between time-setting and time-study. I am not a prophet. I am only a student of the Bible. If 1994 comes and goes without the fulfillments I anticipate, I will review my conclusions again and make the necessary changes. I do not know why this process is so scary to religious people, automobile makers do it every year!

During 1994 or 1995, I anticipate the great earthquake of Revelation 8:2-5 and the beginning of the seven trumpets which are described in Revelation 8. Even though this is June, 1994, the idea that these events are so close is sobering to me. As I said in Chapter 1, time will soon tell if my conclusions are wrong. I would be pleased to discover that my understanding of the seven trumpets is wrong and that my expectations about the future are completely unwarranted. Have you ever faced things you did not want to believe?

Four intersections

Four Bible themes suggest that 1994 could be a significant year. They are:

Seven Millenniums
Seventy Jubilee Cycles
The Daily Intercession of Christ
Revelation's Time Periods Complement 1994

Each of these themes is incomplete within itself as it relates to 1994. So, as I attempt to explain each one of them, understand that they do not stand alone. However, when they are brought together in the final summary, there is a surprising harmony from the sum of all the parts. Holes or gaps within one line of thought are filled with information from an other line. So, do your best to withhold your conclusions until you have reached the summary of this appendix. Then, watch how the four themes come together to affirm that 1994 could be an important year for every person on earth.

Bible Theme #1 — Seven Millenniums

When God created the world, He established three units of time. These units of time are precisely marked by planetary cycles. Notice their duration:

A day = one complete rotation of Earth on its axis

A lunar month = one complete orbit of the moon around Earth

A solar year = one complete orbit of Earth around the sun

The Bible indicates that the daily, monthly and yearly cycles have been known since creation. (Genesis 1:14, 7:11)

After establishing these units of time, God also created a unique time cycle for man that does not have a direct relationship with the three planetary cycles. In fact, in all of God's creation, only human beings are aware of this timing mechanism. All of nature is oblivious to it! This unit of time is called the week.

The mathematical problem with the week is that a cycle of seven days does not wholly fit within the larger cycles of months and years. At first glance, the weekly cycle seems odd, out of place and unnatural within celestial order. Notice the problem:

1 week   = 7 days

4.21 weeks   = 1 lunar month which requires 29 days, 12 hours,
                 43 minutes, 12 seconds

52.17 weeks = 1 solar year which requires 365 days, 5 hours,
                 48 minutes, 46 seconds

Think about this data for a moment. It would have been just as easy for God to make a lunar month of 28.0 days (exactly 4 weeks) instead of 29.53 days. Further, it would have been just as easy for Him to make a solar year of 336.0 days (exactly 48 weeks) instead of 365.252 days. A listener at one of my lectures blurted out, "Yeah, and if He had done that, I would have lost two pay checks each year." Regardless, my point is that God *purposefully* established these timing intervals at Creation.

The weekly cycle

The weekly cycle only exists in the mind of man. It is not tangible nor does anything in nature recognize its existence. It does not fit into any planetary motion. So what is the purpose of the week? Why did God create it? Because God foreknew the existence of sin at the creation of the world, He created a multi-purpose vehicle called the week to accomplish three things as time passed:

1. Special time with God

The weekly cycle was created for man's benefit, and therefore God crowned the weekly cycle with the seventh-day Sabbath. The Sabbath was given to Adam and Eve as the most valuable present that our Creator could provide. He made the seventh day separate and distinct from the other six. He made the seventh day holy — a day of rest, renewal and re-creation. (Genesis

2:1-4) God's original intent for the seventh day was very special. Since human beings could not leave their planet and fly to other realms of the universe, God Himself would come to this tiny speck of a planet on a weekly basis and spend time here with His children, face to face. What condescension!

2. A memorial to Creation

Then sin entered the picture. As a result, the original purpose of the seventh day was modified because the Sabbath quickly lost much of its significance among men. Tainted and corrupted by the degenerate power of sin, Cain and those like him wanted nothing to do with God. They did not want to worship God on His Sabbath. Their rebellion led them to think that they could tell God how He was to be worshiped.

Consequently, the descendants of Adam and Eve who worshiped on the seventh-day Sabbath were few. To these few, the whole world is indebted for the perpetuity of the weekly cycle. For nearly 6,000 years the weekly cycle and the seventh-day Sabbath have been observed. Isn't it strange that 99% of the people living on the face of earth today recognize the existence of the weekly cycle, but only a handful of people recognize the crown-jewel of the week, the seventh-day Sabbath, as God's holy day? How can the knowledge of one be separated from the observance of the other? This is a mystery.

The observance of the special seventh-day Sabbath has singularly kept the knowledge of the weekly cycle intact. Without the Sabbath there is nothing to end or close the week. But, more importantly, the seventh-day Sabbath is man's only memorial of creation week. Notice how this works. If the seventh-day Sabbath of God is denied, then the sixth-day creation of man must also be denied. Without divine revelation about his origin or purpose, man is left without a Maker, and like children without parents, there is no accountability to a greater authority.

The perpetual denial of the seventh-day Sabbath has separated man from the knowledge of God. As a result, we now have a system of science based on the denial of an omnipotent Creator. This science is called evolution. The essential premise behind evolution is that man did not come from the hands of God on the sixth day. Evolutionists have vainly tried to explain the origin of man, but even if they could, they still lack the greater explanation: What is the purpose and meaning of life? On the other hand, creation not only explains the origin of man, it explains the purpose and meaning of life. God's purpose for man is a continual development of character so that man might exhibit the wonderful qualities of his Creator.

Like the antediluvians of Noah's day, much of our civilization today has been led to deny the existence of God's creations. In so doing, the claims of God have also been denied. Evolutionists may have fancy explanations about our origins, but here is one question they cannot explain: Where did the weekly cycle come from, and why is it so universal?

Time has not been lost

Some people argue that the weekly cycle has been lost or manipulated down through the millenniums, making it impossible to know if the current seventh-day Sabbath is the same day that occurred at creation. The problem set forth by this question is easy to resolve.

According to the Bible, Noah entered the ark on the 17th day of the second month during his 600th year. (Genesis 7:11) The Bible also tells us that Noah exited the ark on the 27th day of the second month during his 601st year. (Genesis 8:13,14) These two verses demonstrate that the antediluvians kept a close record (even down to the day) of the passage of time.

About 1,000 years after the Flood, the Israelites left Egypt. They soon discovered that all their food was gone. They complained to Moses and Aaron who, in turn, spoke with the Lord about it. Soon, God sent manna from Heaven. Each week He sent manna on six days, and on the seventh day, He sent none. For 40 years God sustained the nutritional needs of Israel by sending food from Heaven. The point here is that God Himself, approximately 2,500 years after creation, confirmed which day of the week was the seventh day by the absence of food. If there had been any doubt as to which day was the seventh, the absence of food removed all doubt. (It is interesting to note that the Israelites already kept a seven-day calendar even before this demonstration! Compare Exodus 12:2 with Leviticus 25:8.)

About 1,500 years after the Exodus, Jesus Himself walked on earth. He confirmed that what the Jews called the seventh day was, indeed, the seventh-day Sabbath of creation. (See Mark 2:27,28 and Luke 4:16.) If there had been any error on this point, He would have made it known. I find it particularly beautiful that Jesus, the Author of our salvation, rested in His tomb during the hours of the seventh-day Sabbath. He, who experienced the second death for our sins, rested from His ministry of redemption on that wonderful but dark day. Therefore, we can conclude that the Sabbath and the weekly cycle were not lost between Creation and the time of Jesus. One question remains: How can we know if the weekly cycle has remained intact since the days of Jesus?

Diverse religions confirm

Suppose you came to earth on a spaceship and you met three religious leaders. The first person was a Moslem, the second, a Jew and the last, a Christian. You ask each person the same question: "What day of the week do you worship on?" The Moslem would say, "The sixth day, or Friday." The Jew would say, "The seventh day, or Saturday." The Christian would say, "I go to church on Sunday, the first day of the week because of Christ's resurrection."

As you leave earth in your spaceship, you marvel at an interesting point. These three religious bodies represent 50% of earth's inhabitants, and each religious body claims to hold the truth about God. Each religious system also declares that the other two religious systems are false — and yet, they unwittingly confirm something larger than all their claims combined! Their diversity confirms that the weekly cycle remains intact. Here's how: The sixth day is adjacent to the seventh day which is adjacent to the first day of the week. In other words, each religious system worships on unique days that are adjacent to each other. This fact confirms the perpetuity of creation's week since Jesus was on earth and shows that the weekly cycle has not been altered. The Israelites have formally worshiped on the seventh day since the Exodus in 1437 B.C. Christians in Rome, according to Justin Martyr, have formally worshiped on the first day of the week since A.D. 150, and Moslems have formally worshiped on the sixth day of the week since the sixth century A.D. If the weekly cycle had been altered, the holy days of worship would not be adjacent! So, the weekly cycle has not been altered. The seventh day is still God's holy day just as it was at creation.

3. The week as a template

God's memorial to Creation is barely recognized among the billions of people on earth. However, the weekly cycle and the Sabbath will serve one final purpose. This purpose is about to be revealed to mankind. The weekly cycle will convince many that the end is near and at the same time, it will cause global interest in God's holy day.

Bible students have long anticipated an end to sin. The Bible says that a time is coming when sin will be destroyed. (Isaiah 51:6) Since this is true, we know that God has set a limit for the duration of sin. What is that limit? Is it 7,000 years?

I am convinced that from the first day of creation, the purpose of time has been to mark the fulfillment of God's purposes. God foreknew the existence of sin. When He made the weekly cycle, He gave us a "veiled" clue about the timing of His purposes. After all, of what value is time within the dimension of timeless eternity?

This brings up an important question. Do you think the 1,000 years of Revelation 20 is a random number of years or is it a *designed* period of time? For reasons that will be explained in the next section, I believe that the millennium of Revelation 20 is the seventh and final millennium. It is a millennium of rest from sin's existence! In short, it appears that the weekly cycle, unnatural to any celestial movement, is a template of the amount of time that God has allotted for the plan of redemption. The weekly cycle is like a time capsule revealing God's forbearance with the existence of sin and the seventh millennium will be His Sabbath of rest!

With the Lord, a day is like a thousand years

The six days of God's work at Creation seem to parallel the 6,000 years of sin's work of destruction. In Creation's case, as God moved toward the seventh day, His creative works became more beautiful, complex and intricate.

Life forms became more intelligent. In fact, the Sabbath can only be appreciated and understood by the highest living form of creation: man.

Sin has a similar, negative effect. As we move toward the seventh millennium, sin becomes more destructive, complicated and intricate. Man cannot extricate himself from his own problems. The more sinful and degenerate man becomes, the less he appreciates and understands the will of his Maker.

Contrast the differences. One process is noble and beautiful. The other is degenerate and despicable. The real beauty behind the parallel is this: God's Sabbath of rest remains. Whether it is understood or not, God's holy Sabbath cannot be rescinded or made void by man. In fact, the seventh millennium will be a Sabbatical rest for the saints from the cancer of sin. (Hebrews 4) Understand that sin is not destroyed at the second coming. No, sin is not finally destroyed until the end of the seventh millennium when God sends fire down out of heaven and burns up the wicked. (Revelation 20:15)

We may learn certain things about God by studying nature. For instance, we have calculated the length of a day, lunar months and solar years. But without direct revelation from God, man could not know about the cycle of the week or its crown-jewel, God's Sabbath.

The 6,000th year

When does the 6,000th year occur? No one knows for sure and the Bible does not resolve this question. What we can do is to review the genealogies of the Bible and work backwards to determine the approximate time of creation. But, this has problems, too. Early manuscripts vary on genealogies and years. So, at worst, it is a guessing game. At best, it is very interesting. However, I suspect there is evidence enough to know the "time zone" of the 6,000th year. It appears that 1998 is a good candidate for the 6,000th year for several reasons. These reasons will be summarized later. Just keep in mind that one set of possibilities is not trustworthy. However, if the weight of evidence keeps producing the same general numbers, we may be close to knowing where we are in God's plan. The following genealogy is recorded in Genesis 5:1-32; 7:11; and 11:1-32:

Creation to Flood to Exodus

Father	Son	Age	
1. Adam	Seth	130	
2. Seth	Enosh	105	
3. Enosh	Kenan	90	
4. Kenan	Mahalalel	70	
5. Mahalalel	Jared	65	
6. Jared	Enoch	162	
7. Enoch	Methuselah	65	
8. Methuselah	Lamech	187	
9. Lamech	Noah	182	
10. Noah	The Flood	600	2426 B.C.
	Total years ——	**1,646 - 1656****	
11. The Flood	Arphaxad	2	
12. Arphaxad	Shelah	35	
13. Shelah	Eber	30	
14. Eber	Peleg	34	
15. Peleg	Reu	30	
16. Reu	Serug	32	
17. Serug	Nahor	30	
18. Nahor	Terah	29	
19. Terah	Abraham	70	
20. Abraham	Isaac	100	
21. Isaac	Jacob	60	
22. Jacob	Joseph goes to Egypt	107*	
23. Joseph in Egypt	To Exodus	430*	1437 B.C.
	Total years ——	**976 - 989****	

*Jacob was 107 years old when Joseph was taken into Egypt. I believe the 430 years of Exodus 12:41 are dated from Joseph's entry into Egypt as a slave. Some prefer to date the 430 years mentioned in Exodus 12:41 from Abraham's call. (Genesis 12:1) If the latter position is correct, and the date of the Exodus is 1437 B.C., then creation would be dated between 3890 and 3920 B.C. and the 6,000th year would occur between A.D. 2110-2140.

**A range of years is given because it is highly unlikely that each generation was born on the birthday of his ancestor. For example, ten generations could have a maximum cumulative error of almost ten years.

Exodus dating

For reasons to be explained, I find only one date that can satisfy the date of the Exodus. It appears to be 1437 B.C. If this date is not correct, then it has to be increased or decreased by units of 49 years because of the operation of the Jubilee calendar units. If 1437 B.C. is indeed true, and if the genealogical numbers in the Hebrew Pentateuch are trustworthy (allowing for cumulative error), the creation of the world could have occurred about 4072 B.C.

> 1437 B.C. — The Exodus
> +   984* years from the Exodus back to the Flood
> + 1651* years from the Flood back to Adam's creation
> 4072 B.C. — The Creation

*Cumulative error averaged

Those individuals who have investigated this subject will recognize that certain assumptions go with the 4072 B.C. date. If the Bible account reflects the fact that offspring were not born on the same day and month each year, and if no one is missing in the lineage, then 4072 B.C. could represent the approximate year of Adam and Eve's creation.

The Bible is also silent on the length of time that Adam and Eve were in the Garden of Eden before their expulsion. However, we do know that Cain and Abel were born *after* their expulsion from Eden. We also know that their third son, Seth, was born when Adam and Eve were 130 years old. These sparse facts combine to render the following possibility:

Adam and Eve were created about 4072 B.C.
Adam and Eve lived in the Garden of Eden about 70 years before sinning.
A year or so after their expulsion, Cain was born and shortly afterwards,
    Abel was born.
When Cain and Abel were in their 30's, Cain killed Abel.
Eve conceived and replaced the loss of Abel. Seth was born when
    Adam and Eve were 130 years old.

If the above is reasonable, then sin would have occurred around 4002 B.C. This time frame complements the possibility that 1998 could be very close to the 6,000th year. If we have actually passed the 6,000th year of sin, the seventh-millennium Sabbatical theory would not make any sense. However, since the Bible is favorable to the possibility that we have not reached the 6,000th year yet, this is worthy of exploration.

A future Sabbath Rest is promised

Notice these verses: **"For forty years I was angry with that generation; I said, 'They are a people whose hearts go astray, and they have not known my ways.' So I declared on oath in my anger, 'They shall never enter my rest.' "** (Psalms 95:10-11) Why does God call the promised land "my rest"? What is the connection between the Sabbath-rest and the promised land in the book of Hebrews?

This text is important to our study because the promised land symbolizes God's seventh-day Sabbath-rest. In other words, the weekly rest of the seventh day was a sample of the joy that would be found for years to come in the promised land. But, the first generation of Israelites did not enter God's rest. Fifteen hundred years after the Exodus, the apostle Paul understood that the Sabbath-rest of the *eternal* promised land was still future. Notice what he said, **"There remains, then, a Sabbath-rest for the people of God; for anyone who enters God's rest also rests from his own work, just as God did from his. Let us, therefore, make every effort**

to enter that rest, so that no one will fall by following their example
of disobedience." (Hebrews 4:9-11)

Does the Sabbath-rest of the promised land, spoken of by Paul, occur during
the seventh millennium? It seems so because a Sabbath-rest is directly related
to God's seventh-day Sabbath. My guess is that the seventh millennium
will start right on time, just as the seventh-day Sabbath starts on time each
week.

We leave this section with some thoughts unfinished. The threads will be
picked up in the summary.

Bible Theme #2 — Seventy Jubilee Cycles

Because God is neither shallow nor mindless about the things He creates,
we should carefully consider the calendar He introduced to Israel just before
the Exodus. This calendar is often called the Jubilee calendar. It is built
upon a square template of the weekly cycle. It is a matrix of seven 7's
totaling 49 years. Look at the matrix below and notice that it is one week
wide and seven weeks deep (7 by 7):

God's Calendar

Sun	Mon	Tue	Wed	Thu	Fri	Sab	
1	2	3	4	5	6	7	Week 1
8	9	10	11	12	13	14	Week 2
15	16	17	18	19	20	21	Week 3
22	23	24	25	26	27	28	Week 4
29	30	31	32	33	34	35	Week 5
36	37	38	39	40	41	42	Week 6
43	44	45	46	47	48	49	Week 7

Now, notice how our calendar and God's calendar compare:

Our Calendar		God's Calendar	
1 Decade =	10 Years	1 Week =	7 Years
10 Decades =	100 Years	7 Weeks =	49 Years
100 Years =	1 Century	49 Years =	1 Jubilee Cycle

God's Calendar

The Jubilee calendar is important. A basic understanding of this calendar is necessary to appreciate why it points to 1994.

In the Jubilee calendar, each day of the week represents a year. The Jubilee calendar was implemented just before the Exodus, in the Spring of the year, and it marks the passage of time by counting weeks of years. (Exodus 12:1,2) This may sound complicated, but remember, the Jews did not use a fixed date to mark their calendars like we do today.

When a person speaks of 1994 (January - December), to what is he referring? He is saying that there have been 1,994 years since the birth of Jesus (actually, 1,994 is not the actual number of years, but this is beside the point for now). Because our calendar dates from an event that is recognized by most nations of the world, we can keep track of years quite easily. But suppose the Japanese did not base the date of their calendar on the birth of Jesus, what year automobile would Honda be selling right now?

In ancient times each nation adopted its own calendar so that time was often referred to like this: **"In the 15th year of the reign of Tiberius Caesar...."** (Luke 3:1) In those times, there were multitudes of small nations and no common calendar, so it was almost impossible to date an event. Pompous kings liked to have time dated according to their rule, but unfortunately, they were mortal and every time a new king ascended the throne, the calendar started over. You can imagine the problems that ancient historians had. Even worse, you can imagine the problems that modern historians have as they try to date events from the past. For these and other reasons, precision dating of ancient events by archeological records is very difficult.

The weekly cycle is a template

God foreknew the problems Israel would face in trying to keep track of time, so He created a calendar *based on the template* of the weekly cycle. He gave this calendar to Israel at the time of the Exodus and He required them to faithfully observe it. To prevent Israel from dismissing the importance of His divine calendar, God declared that regular events were to happen at certain times.

The Sabbatical

God declared that after Israel entered the land that He was going to give them, the land itself must observe a Sabbath of rest every seventh year. (Leviticus 25:3-7) Every seventh year, the land was to lay fallow. It was not to be planted or harvested. In His divine wisdom, God accomplished two important things with the seventh-year Sabbatical. First, the observance of the Sabbatical would ever keep the importance of His weekly seventh day Sabbath intact. Second and more importantly, God wanted to test Israel's faith every seventh year. He wanted to see if they would trust Him and observe His Sabbath years. Some people have claimed that the Sabbatical was for the benefit of the land; however, the facts clearly dispute this claim. Consider this: The sixth or last year of the harvest cycle produced more food than other years! (Leviticus 25:21) In other words, the largest crop took place *after* the soil had been producing for five consecutive years.

The Jubilee year

The 49th year of a Jubilee cycle was a high Sabbatical because it was the seventh Sabbath of the cycle. The 49th year was then followed by the once-per-generation Jubilee year. The Jubilee year was a Sabbatical year also, and it was a celebration of a completed Jubilee cycle just like a wedding anniversary is a celebration of a completed year.

This may sound strange, but the 50th year celebration took place during the first year of a new cycle. For this reason, some people are confused about the length of a Jubilee cycle, but God provides a simple solution to the question. The solution is found in the Feast of Pentecost. The Feast of Pentecost occurred on the 50th day after seven seventh-day Sabbaths had passed. (Leviticus 23:15,16) Thus, the 50th day of Pentecost always occurred on the *first* day of the week. In like manner, the 50th year celebration occurred during the *first* year of the new Jubilee cycle. In addition to this point, the unbroken weekly cycle of years definitely confirms that Jubilee cycles were to be reckoned as adjacent units of seven weeks containing 49 years.

During the Jubilee year, God required that all real estate debts be canceled and that all land be returned to its original owner. (Homes within cities were excluded.) God did this to remind each generation that the land they possessed was not theirs but His. (See Leviticus 25:23 and Jeremiah 2:7.) He wanted them to know that they did not earn or deserve the land, but that He had given it to them because He loved them. (It is still the same today. The saints who inherit the New Earth will know that they do not deserve the land, but it comes as a gift from God.) One last point, the Jews were not to plant or harvest their fields during the Jubilee year, for it was a holy Sabbatical year to the Lord just like the Sabbatical years. (Leviticus 25:11,12)

The meaning of rest

So, we have learned three things. First, the seventh-year Sabbatical rest for the land was a test to see if Israel would rest from their labor and trust in God to supply their needs. Second, the Jubilee year was an extra special test of faith because two Sabbatical years occurred consecutively. Even more, they had to return all property outside the cities to its original owners. Finally, the observance of these events were designed to keep the observance of the Jubilee cycle intact.

Notice the intimate relationship in God's calendar surrounding the Sabbath. The observance of the seventh-day Sabbath kept the weekly cycle intact, and the observance of the Sabbatical years kept the weeks of years intact which in turn kept the Jubilee cycles intact.

Consider the following about the Jubilee calendar: With the exception of the first Jubilee cycle, a Jubilee cycle contains *eight* Sabbatical years: seven seventh-year Sabbaticals plus the first year which is the Jubilee year Sabbatical. Also notice that the next Jubilee cycle continues without interrupting the weekly cycle. Last, notice that any Sabbatical year is always a function of seven. For example, the Sabbatical year for Week 4 is year number 28. (7 x 4 = 28)

Sun	Mon	Tue	Wed	Thu	Fri	Sab	
50/1	2	3	4	5	6	**7**	Week 1
8	9	10	11	12	13	**14**	Week 2
15	16	17	18	19	20	**21**	Week 3
22	23	24	25	26	27	**28**	Week 4
29	30	31	32	33	34	**35**	Week 5
36	37	38	39	40	41	**42**	Week 6
43	44	45	46	47	48	**49**	Week 7
			Next	**Cycle**			
50/1	2	3	4	5	6	**7**	Week 1
8	9	10	11	12	13	**14**	Week 2
15	16	17	18	19	20	**21**	Week 3

Warning

What God makes holy, He declares important to man. God does not allow man to treat His holy things with contempt and remain guiltless. Therefore, God's punishment for willfully trampling on His holy things is very serious. God warns human beings of His wrath if they ignore His commands. Understand that if a person tramples on God's holy Sabbath without knowing that he is doing wrong, God does not hold that person accountable. But, if a person refuses to recognize, admit or learn of God's holy Sabbath, sooner or later he will find himself in serious trouble. And, sad to say, this was the experience of Israel.

When God gave Israel the Jubilee calendar, He made clear their responsibility. He warned, **"But if you will not listen to me and carry out all these commands, and if you reject my decrees and abhor my laws and fail to carry out all my commands and so violate my covenant, then I will do this to you: I will bring upon you sudden terror, wasting diseases** and fever that will destroy your sight and drain away your life. You will plant seed in vain, because your enemies will eat it... I will lay waste the land, so that your enemies who live there will be appalled. I will scatter you among the nations and will draw out my sword and pursue you. Your land will be laid waste, and your cities will lie in ruins. Then the land will enjoy its sabbath years all the time that it lies desolate and you are in the country of your enemies; then the land will rest and enjoy its sabbaths. All the time that it lies desolate, the land will have the rest it did not have during the sabbaths you lived in it." (Leviticus 26:14-35)

If we look carefully at the penalty for violating the Sabbatical years, we may correctly estimate their value in God's sight. *The penalty for violating the Sabbatical years was severe because God wanted Israel to live by faith. He also wanted Israel to perpetuate His calendar.* Since the Jubilee calendar was initiated just before the Exodus (Exodus 12:2), God designed that Israel should date their beginning as a nation at the Exodus. Indeed, the annual Passover services would ever remind them of their benevolent Creator.

Jubilees are in the Bible

The silence of Sabbatical or Jubilee celebrations in the Bible leads me to conclude that Israel did not measure up to God's ideal for long. In fact, there is only one Jubilee mentioned in all the Bible. It is mentioned twice: Isaiah 37:30 and 2 Kings 19:29. (An oblique reference is found in Ezekiel 7:13) Also, the seventh year Sabbatical is mentioned twice, once in Jeremiah 34 and in Nehemiah 10.

God's patience and long-suffering with Israel's backsliding is beyond human understanding. For centuries He tried to get Israel to shape up and accomplish all that He had in mind, but they refused. Eventually, Israel filled up its cup of iniquity. Oddly enough, the full cup was reached when Israel violated 70 Sabbatical years.

When 70 violated Sabbaticals were reached, Israel was summarily expelled from Jerusalem and hauled off to Babylon by King Nebuchadnezzar. Israel had to remain in Babylon for 70 years because the land had missed 70 Sabbatical years of rest! Remember God's warning? **"All the time that it** lies desolate, the land will have the rest it did not have during the sabbaths you lived in it." (Leviticus 26:35) In other words, God's patience with Israel reached its limit with 70 Sabbatical year violations and He had them evicted from the land. Notice what the Bible says about their captivity: **"The land enjoyed its sabbath rests; all the time of its desolation it rested, until the seventy years were completed in fulfillment of the word of the Lord spoken by Jeremiah."** (2 Chronicles 36:21)

Day/Year

Earlier it was demonstrated how a day in the Jubilee calendar represents a literal year. Notice how this was confirmed to Israel through the prophet Ezekiel about 592 B.C.: **"Now, son of man, take a clay tablet, put it in front of you and draw the city of Jerusalem on it. Then lay siege to it: Erect siege works against it, build a ramp up to it, set up camps against it and put battering rams around it. Then take an iron pan, place it as an iron wall between you and the city and turn your face toward it. It will be under siege, and you shall besiege it. This will be a sign to the house of Israel. Then lie on your left side and put the sin of the house of Israel upon yourself. You are to bear their sin for the number of days you lie on your side. I have assigned you the same number of days as the years of their sin. So for 390 days you will bear the sin of the house of Israel. After you have finished this, lie down again, this time on your right side, and bear the sin of the house of Judah. I have assigned you 40 days, a day for each year."** (Ezekiel 4:1-6)

Notice how the math proves that a Jubilee cycle contains 49 years. If we add the 390 years of Israel with the 40 offending years of Judah, we obtain a total of 430 years of sinful living. This is why Ezekiel had to lay on his right and left sides for a total of 430 days — a day for each year. In 430 years, there are eight complete Jubilee cycles plus a partial cycle (the 9th) which contains 38 years. The amazing point here is that 430 years contain exactly 70 Sabbaticals! (Keep in mind that there are 8 Sabbaticals in a Jubilee cycle of 49 years.) Here's how the total of 70 Sabbaticals is found:

430 Years Contain 70 Sabbaticals

Jubilee Cycle	Years	Sabbaticals
1	49	8
2	49	8
3	49	8
4	49	8
5	49	8
6	49	8
7	49	8
8	49	8
9	38	6
Total	430	70

It is also interesting to notice that when the 70 years of captivity had been paid in full, notice what the Lord did: **"In the first year of Cyrus king of Persia, in order to fulfill the word of the Lord spoken by Jeremiah,** *the Lord moved the heart* **of Cyrus king of Persia to make a proclamation throughout his realm and to put it in writing: "This is what Cyrus king of Persia says: "'The Lord, the God of heaven, has given me all the kingdoms of the earth and he has appointed me to build a temple for him at Jerusalem in Judah. Anyone of his people among you—may the Lord his God be with him, and let him go up.'"** (2 Chronicles 36:22,23; emphasis mine)

God is timely

This point fascinates me. God did not forget His people in Babylon. He moved on the heart of King Cyrus to set His people free at the right time!

This point is underscored again in the Old Testament. Notice the specifics: Israel left Egypt on the 15th day of the first month of their first year. (Numbers 33:3) Then, two years later, Israel's faith stumbled at Kadesh Barnea when they sent the spies into the promised land. There, God's anger burned against them and that generation died in the wilderness. God promised them 40 years of desert living! (Numbers 14:34) Then, when the 40 years were completed, Israel entered the promised land on the 15th day of the first month during the 41st year — 40 years to the very day after leaving Egypt! (Joshua 5:10,11)

Now, an important point has to be made. As far as God was concerned, the Jubilee calendar began two weeks before the Exodus. This is proven by the fact that when God punished the Israelites at Kadesh Barnea with 40 years in the wilderness, He did not count the 40 years from Kadesh Barnea; rather, He counted from 15th day of the first month of the year of the Exodus. (Deuteronomy 2:14) So, the punch line is this: God applied the day for a year principle at Kadesh Barnea because the Jubilee calendar, which establishes the day/year principle was already in operation.

This little point is critical to correctly dating the Jubilee calendar. In other words, people can only be as certain of the termination of the calendar as they are of the commencement of the calendar.

Day/Year again

While in Babylonian captivity, God spoke to the prophet Daniel and told him that He was going to give Israel another chance. This opportunity, would again have a limit of 70 units. However, instead of granting Israel 70 Sabbaticals of mercy, God moved the next larger unit within the calendar. He granted Israel 70 sevens (70 weeks of years). This, God offered, would be enough time for Israel to straighten up and become all that He wanted. Note the incremental progression within the Jubilee calendar. We move from 40 day/years in the wilderness to 70 Sabbaticals/years in Babylon to 70 weeks/years in Jerusalem. Did you notice the increasing increments moving from days to Sabbaticals to weeks? God has a very important purpose in this progression. (Remember my assertion that sin would last 7,000 years? In other words, the period of time allotted for sin appears to be 70 centuries!)

70 weeks are consecutive

70 weeks in the Jubilee calendar contain 490 literal years. Here's how:

1 week contains 7 years
70 weeks of 7 years = 70 x 7 = 490 literal years

Toward the end of the Babylonian captivity, God told Daniel that He was going to grant 70 weeks of Jubilee time for Israel to put away sin and bring in everlasting righteousness. God also told Daniel that the 70 weeks would begin with the issuing of a decree to restore and rebuild Jerusalem. Finally, God told Daniel that Messiah would appear after 69 weeks had expired and in the middle of the 70th week, Messiah would be "cut off" and confirm the covenant of salvation. (Daniel 9:24-27) The events occurred right on time just as God predicted!

Briefly, here are the historical facts. Around the first day of the first month in the Jubilee year of 457 B.C. (our March 19 or 20 — the Spring equinox), Artaxerxes issued a decree granting the restoration of Jerusalem and the temple. Ezra knew the decree was coming, and he began preparing on the first day of the first month of the year. He finally left Babylon with the decree in hand on the 12th day of the first month (Ezra 8:31) and arrived in Jerusalem on the 1st day of the fifth month (our July/August) (Ezra 7:9).

The timing of the king's decree, issued during the first few days of the first month of 457 B.C., was not coincidental. God moved on the heart of Artaxerxes to write the restoration decree just as the Jubilee year was beginning that Spring. *Right on time* the king issued the decree. You should not be surprised, for the Bible says that God moved on the heart of King Cyrus to write the release from Babylon *right on time*. (2 Chronicles 36:22)

Since God's calendar operates from Spring equinox to Spring equinox, the 69 weeks predicted in Daniel's prophecy expired in the Spring of A.D. 27 as the 70th and final week of seven years began. During that first year of the 70th week, A.D. 27, Jesus was baptized and began His ministry. (A.D. 27 is the Sunday year of the 70th week. A.D. 28 was the Monday year, etc.) Luke 3 pinpoints the historical location saying, **"In the fifteenth year of the reign of Tiberius Caesar—when Pontius Pilate was governor of Judea, Herod tetrarch of Galilee, his brother Philip tetrarch of Iturea and Traconitis, and Lysanias tetrarch of Abilene— {2} during the high priesthood of Annas and Caiaphas, the word of God came to John son** of Zechariah in the desert. {21} When all the people were being baptized, Jesus was baptized too.... {23} Now Jesus himself was about thirty years old when he began his ministry. He was the son, so it was thought, of Joseph, the son of Heli." (Luke 3:1-23)

Note: Some Bible students claim that the Jubilee calendar operates from Fall to Fall. This is not the case. It is true that the Jews observed a Fall to Fall *civil* calendar after the Babylonian captivity, but the Jubilee calendar dates from the Exodus, a full 800 years *before* the Babylonian captivity.

The prophecy of Daniel indicates that Messiah would be "cut off" in the middle of the 70th week. Notice how the weekly cycle of years pinpoint the year of Christ's death as A.D. 30. Remember, a Jubilee year begins in the Spring. So, the Sunday year began in the Spring of A.D. 27 and the Wednesday year is the middle year of the week. Jesus died on the 14th day of the first month in A.D. 30, at the time of Passover:

The 70th Week

Sun	Mon	Tue	Wed	Thu	Fri	Sab
27	28	29	30	31	32	33

While the historical and prophetic harmony of these matters is impressive and most interesting to investigate, there is a larger matter taking place that we need to be aware of. *The ministry and death of Jesus confirms the synchronism of the day/years within the 70th week.* Surely, the words of Paul make a lot of sense: **"But when the time had fully come, God sent his Son, born of a woman, born under law."** (Galatians 4:4)

Try to understand this point. The weekly cycle of years is an unbroken chain just like the weekly cycle of days is an unbroken chain. When Jesus came to earth, He confirmed which year is the Sunday year or first year of the weekly cycle (A.D. 27) and which year is the Wednesday year, the middle year of the weekly cycle (A.D. 30). Once we know the synchronism of the years (which day of the week is which), we discover a number of other things about timing that would be otherwise unknown.

For example, we discover that the decree of Artaxerxes was issued in a Jubilee year (70 weeks equals 10 Jubilees). Further, the Jubilee year in 457 B.C. correctly synchronizes with Hezekiah's 15th year — the only Jubilee year mentioned in the Bible!

Using the unbroken chain of the week of years, we can also pinpoint the seventh-year under discussion in Jeremiah 34:12-21 as 591 B.C. because this would be the *only* Sabbatical year within Zedekiah's reign of 11 years.

The beauty of knowing the synchronism of the week of years is that we are able to chronologically locate events that cannot otherwise be known for sure. Once the reader understands the operation of God's Jubilee calendar, the chronology of events becomes much clearer and more forceful.

It is a sad footnote to reveal that when the 70 weeks were fully expired (A.D. 33), the Jews had not cooperated with God as He desired. Israel had willfully rebelled against His own Son; so, in A.D. 70, God sent the Romans to Jerusalem and it was destroyed.

7 x 10 = 70 = The End?

Have you noticed that God's patience may be measured in units of 70? If you are a student of the Old Testament, you know that judgment day, the most important day in the sanctuary service, was the Day of Atonement. It occurred on the 10th day of the seventh month. You may have already thought about the possibility that the total existence of sin will be 7,000 years, which just happens to be 70 centuries. I also find it more than coincidental that, the length of life itself is often called threescore and ten, which is 70. My point is that the number seven represents a complete or full number, and the number 10 appears to represent a magnification of the number. When the two numbers are multiplied, the resulting 70 appears to be the limit of God's patience.

Kindness has a limit

"Then Peter came to Jesus and asked, 'Lord, how many times shall I forgive my brother when he sins against me? Up to seven times?' Jesus answered, 'I tell you, not seven times, but seventy-seven times.' "

(Matthew 18:21,22) The NIV translation of this verse seems to say 77 times. Actually, Jesus did not say 77 times. Rather, He turned to Peter and said, "seventy-sevens." Peter immediately understood the phrase. Just as Israel had been forgiven by God and granted seventy-sevens (490 years) of redemptive opportunity, Peter was to forgive his brother and grant him the same compassion.

Prophetic time periods

It is beyond the scope of this chapter to examine all the corporate prophetic time periods in the Bible. However, a point about the fourth apocalyptic rule given on page 8 must be made: *All apocalyptic time periods occurring during the presence of Jubilee cycles are to be interpreted in Jubilee units of time. Under this system, a day represents a literal year.* (An apocalyptic time period is a time period that occurs in one of the 18 apocalyptic prophecies of Daniel and Revelation.) This rule also means that apocalyptic time periods *outside* the operation of Jubilee cycles are to be interpreted as literal units of time. This concept becomes very interesting when we consider the possibility that there could be a finite number of Jubilee cycles. That number could be 70.

Notice how the Jubilee principle works with respect to prophetic time periods. Before Jubilee cycles were given, prophetic time periods were literal. Therefore, Noah's 120 years of warning (Genesis 6:3) were 120 literal years because they happened *before* Jubilee cycles began. The 40 years of wandering in the wilderness followed the day/year principle because the Jubilee calendar began at the time of the Exodus, not with the entrance of Israel into the promised land. (See Deuteronomy 2:14, Numbers 14:34.) The 1,260 days of Daniel 7:25, and Revelation 12:6,14 are Jubilee units so they represent a 1,260 year time period. The 1,000 years of the seventh millennium will be literal years because they occur *after* the expiration of the 70th Jubilee cycle which occurred in the Spring of 1994.

This simple concept clears up several problems regarding time periods in Daniel and Revelation. For example: The 1,335 days of Daniel 12 are literal, the 42 months of Revelation 13:5 are literal and the five months of torture during the fifth trumpet are also literal (Revelation 9:5) because all of these time periods occur after the Jubilee cycles end.

Jubilee cycles after A.D. 70

Two prophecies confirm the perpetuity of Jubilee cycles long after the demise of ancient Israel in A.D 70. The first prophecy is found in Daniel 7:25. Here the Bible says that the little horn power would persecute the saints of God for a time, times and dividing of time. This time period of 1,260 day/years began in A.D. 538 and ended in 1798. History confirms the duration of this time period. Even more, it verifies the presence and operation of the day/year principle long after A.D. 70. Further, the fulfillment of Daniel 7:25 confirms the existence of the Jubilee calendar, for without it, there is no consistent principle which demands the use of the day/year mechanism.

The second prophecy that confirms the perpetuity of the Jubilee cycle long after the demise of ancient Israel is found in Daniel 8:14. Whatever question may have existed about the perpetuity of the Jubilee calendar is eliminated by the fulfillment of this prophecy. Because this prophecy began 457 years before Christ and reaches down to A.D. 1844, two impressive points must be recognized. First, the day/year principle is at work here because the first 10 Jubilee cycles (70 sevens or 490 literal years) granted to Israel are "cut off" from this larger prophecy. In other words, if the 70 sevens are day/years as a result of Jubilee cycles, then the 2,300 days of Daniel 8:14 are day/years because of Jubilee cycles. Second, this prophecy points out that the ministry of Christ in the Heavenly sanctuary is intimately connected to the operation of Jubilee cycles. (The reader is directed to the book *The Revelation of Jesus*, for a deeper explanation of these matters. See the list of study helps at the back of this book.)

How 1437 B.C. is calculated

The calculation of the date of the Exodus is very important. The reason is this: The ending date of the Jubilee calendar can only be established if the beginning date can be identified. In other words, the Spring of 1994 marks the end of 70 Jubilee cycles because Jubilee cycles began in 1437 B.C.! The computation of 1437 B.C. is not complicated but it is somewhat tedious. Here are the five steps necessary to validate the date of the Exodus:

Step 1. God established His calendar-year two weeks before the Exodus by identifying the 1st day - 1st month - 1st year. God's year operates from Spring (equinox) to Spring (equinox). (See Exodus 12:1-12; 40:17.) **(Note:** When I speak of a Jubilee year such as A.D. 33, I am referring to a time period that reaches from March A.D. 33 to March A.D. 34. For simplicity, I call it A.D. 33 because the Jubilee year began in the Spring of Julian A.D. 33 and the bulk of the Jubilee year occurs during that Julian year.)

Step 2. Jesus began His ministry on time (A.D. 27) and He died on time in the middle of the 70th week (A.D. 30) — counting weeks from the decree of Artaxerxes. (See Luke 3 and Daniel 9:27.) Consider this: If weeks of years are counted from their origin at the Exodus, Jesus died in the middle of the 210th week which happens to be the last week in 30 Jubilee cycles.

70th Week							71st Week							Etc.
S	M	T	W	T	F	S	S	M	T	W	T	F	S	
27	28	29	30	31	32	33	34	35	36	37	38	39	40	

Step 3. If A.D. 30 = Wednesday year, then the following is true:

    457 B.C. = Sunday year
    1437 B.C. = Sunday year
    1388 B.C. = Sunday year
    1994 = Sunday year

The 70 weeks prophecy began in the Spring of the Sunday year (457 B.C.) with the decree of Artaxerxes and it ended with the 70th Sabbatical year A.D. 33. A total of 490 years (counting from Spring to Spring) elapsed. The decree by Artaxerxes was issued in the first days of Spring, 457 B.C. (See Ezra 6:19; 7:9 and 8:31.).

Step 4. The Bible identifies the location of a Jubilee year during the 15th year of King Hezekiah. **"In the fourteenth year of King Hezekiah's reign, Sennacherib king of Assyria attacked all the fortified cities of**

Judah and captured them." [Isaiah said to the king] **"This will be the sign for you, O Hezekiah: 'This year [your fourteenth] you will eat what grows by itself, and the second year [your 15th year] what springs from that. But in the third year sow and reap, plant vineyards and eat their fruit.'"** (See Isaiah 36:1, 37:30.)

This Jubilee year sign can be accurately located because king Sennacherib has to be in power and we know that Jubilee years are always Sunday years. A review of history reveals that Sennacherib was in power around 705 B.C. So, the 15th of Hezekiah has to occur after 705 B.C. and the first Sunday year after 705 B.C. is 702 B.C. We can determine if the first Sunday year is the Jubilee year by starting with the well known date of 586 B.C. when Jerusalem was finally destroyed by Nebuchadnezzar, and count backwards through the reign of kings to Hezekiah's 15th year:

		Regnal*	Actual	Date
1.	Hezekiah**	14	11	702
2.	Manesseh	55	54	692
3.	Amon	2	2	638
4.	Josiah	31	29	636
5.	Jehoiakim	11	10	607
6.	Jehoiachin	.25	.25	597
7.	Zedekiah	11	11	596
8.	Jerusalem's 3rd destruction	---		586
	Total	125	118	

*A regnal year is counted as a year on the throne — even if it is only a partial year. A regnal year is also credited to a king even if two kings reign at the same time. For example, David and Solomon (Father - Son) were kings of Israel at the same time. They both reigned 40 regnal years, but the actual number of years they reigned over Israel does not equal 80 years. This is because their reigns ran concurrently for a few years. These were the customs in ancient times. Often, the outgoing king stayed on the throne to stabilize the authority of the incoming king if he was a young heir to the throne.

**In Hezekiah's 14th year, he was given a promise of 15 more years of life — so his total reign would last about 29 years. The Jubilee year occurred during his 15th year on the throne — leaving him about 14 more years of life. I assume that he placed his heir, Manesseh, on the throne when he turned 12 years old to teach him the ways of the court before Hezekiah died (after all, he knew the year of his forthcoming death). Thus, Hezekiah reigned for a total of 29 years, but he reigned alone for about 26 years.

Note: Regnal years for this time-period total 125 while the actual years are 118. The seven years of overlapping is well within the number of years allowed by scholars for this time-period. Many scholars allow 10 years of coregent reign for this list of kings.

Summarizing: From the death of Jesus in the middle year of the 70th week (A.D. 30), we can determine the date of all Sunday years. Hezekiah's 15th year is a Sunday/Jubilee year combination which follows a 49th Sabbatical year. We also know that Hezekiah's 15th year has to occur after Sennacherib comes to power in 705 B.C. One date, 702 B.C., exclusively satisfies the parameters. Other Sunday years are either too late or too early to meet all of the specifications.

Notice the impact of this conclusion: If 702 B.C. is correctly identified as a Jubilee year, then the decree of Artaxerxes in 457 B.C. is a Jubilee year because it falls on the exact multiple of 49 year cycles with 702 B.C.! When one Jubilee year is known, we can calculate all Jubilee years — forward or backward. For example, A.D. 34 is a Sunday year, and it is a Jubilee year.

Finally, the year of the Exodus is year 1 of the Jubilee calendar. It is a Sunday year because Sunday is the first day/year in the calendar. The Sunday year of the Exodus has to synchronize with 702 B.C., 457 B.C., the 70 weeks, and of course, the 70th week. Good news, it does!

Step 5. The last step is to locate the reign of Solomon because we can leapfrog from the year of the Exodus to the fourth year of Solomon. **"In the four hundred and eightieth year after the Israelites had come out of Egypt, in the fourth year of Solomon's reign over Israel, in the**

month of Ziv, the second month, he began to build the temple of the Lord." (1 Kings 6:1) If we can locate the approximate time of Solomon's reign, we can then determine the exact year of the Exodus because it has to be a Jubilee year. We know that 702 B.C., 457 B.C. and the dates of the 70th week are perfectly synchronized. So, one of the following dates has to be the year of the Exodus because these are 49 year cycles within the era of the Exodus date and the fourth year of Solomon's reign:

1486 B.C.   1437 B.C.   1388 B.C.   1339 B.C.

Providentially, there is well confirmed, widely accepted data outside the Bible showing that Ahab, king of Israel was killed during the 22nd year of his reign in 852 B.C. We also know that the distance between Solomon's 4th year and Ahab's death is a maximum distance of 120 regnal years (turns out to be 106 actual years). Here are the regnal years (as recorded in the Bible) from Solomon's 4th year to Ahab's 22nd year of his reign:

Regnal Years

1. Solomon:	36 years	
2. Jeroboam:	22 years	
3. Nadab:	2 years	
4. Baasha:	24 years	
5. Elah	2 years	
6. Zimri	1 week	
7. Omri	12 years	
8. Ahab	22 years	
Total Regnal Years:	120 years	

If we calculate the date of the Exodus using these regnal years, we find:

The date of Ahab's death:	852 B.C.
Plus regnal years back to Solomon:	120
Plus 480 back to Exodus:	480
Date of the Exodus:	**1452 B.C.**

But, 1452 B.C. is not a Jubilee year nor is 1452 a Sunday year. Moving forward to the closest Jubilee year because regnal years always total more than actual years, we find:

The date of Ahab's death: 852 B.C.
Add 106 actual years: 106 (reducing regnal years by 14)
Add 480 back to Exodus: 480

Date of the Exodus: **1437 B.C.**

The difference between regnal and actual years for Solomon and Ahab is 14. This is well within the tolerance allowed for the succession of eight kings. Some scholars reduce the regnal years for this time period by five and say the actual years are 115 instead of 106. But, the records of coregent reigns during this time-period are non-existent. So, the actual years must remain within the realm of educated guessing. However, the Jubilee calendar imposes a "timing matrix" on this time period. Here's why: The Exodus has to occur during a Jubilee year (Sunday year). Second, the span of time between the Exodus and Solomon/Ahab has to begin with Jubilee calendar year one and conclude in 852 B.C. Finally, the Bible limits the span of time between Solomon and Ahab to 120 regnal years. So, 1437 B.C. is the only year that can qualify for the Exodus. It is a Sunday year and it is the first year of the Jubilee calendar. In addition, 1437 B.C. occurs within the time-frame allotted by Scripture. All other Jubilee years under consideration are too near or too far away from the regnal or actual reigns of the kings to qualify. Therefore, 1437 B.C. becomes the exclusive date of the Exodus and the expiration of 70 complete Jubilee cycles (3,430 years) occurred at the Spring equinox on March 19, 1994. Incidently, 70 Jubilee cycles equals 490 weeks of years — just like 70 weeks equals 490 years.

If the Jubilee calendar expired in March, 1994, if the future prophetic time-periods of Daniel and Revelation are literal time-periods, and if they commence during 1994 or 1995, can we conclude that 1998 is near the 6,000th year? It appears to be. Even if my assumption that the Great Tribulation time-period will begin in 1994 is off a year or two, this does not change the overall picture because the 6,000th year is out there and we are moving toward it — one day at a time.

The real value of the Jubilee calendar is not the placement of historical events, as helpful as this is. Rather, the beauty of the Jubilee calendar today is that we have a simple but profound explanation of why God reckons some prophecies as a day for a year and others He reckons as literal time. This little key opens up a new world of discovery about the literal timing of end-time events.

Bible Theme #3 — The Daily Intercession of Jesus

Most Christians understand that Jesus is in Heaven, sitting at the right hand of the Father. They also understand that Jesus is our intercessor. He intercedes for us because we are sinful and faulty. (Hebrews 7:25) What most Christians do not realize is that Christ's intercession has two levels of operation. On the corporate level, He intercedes on behalf of our sinful world. On the personal level, He intercedes for me, a sinner. This truth is borne out in three of the Old Testament sanctuary services.

The morning and evening sacrifice

The morning and evening sacrifices were conducted at sunrise and sunset each day. A flawless year-old male lamb was sacrificed on the Altar of Burnt Offering. The priest conducting the service carried the blood into the sanctuary. He then sprinkled some of the lamb's blood on the Altar of Incense and put some blood on the horns of the altar. The service also consisted of burning special incense on coals of the Altar of Incense.

This ritual is often called the "Daily" or "Continual" because it took place every morning and evening. It was through the atoning merits of the "Daily" that Israel could dwell in the presence of God without being destroyed! (See Exodus 29:38-46; 30:7,8.) So understand a vital point: The "Daily" provided **corporate** atonement on behalf of the whole nation of Israel and was not provided for any one individual.

This ritual served as a model of what Jesus has been doing in Heaven since the day Adam and Eve sinned. Every day, moment by moment, Jesus has stood between guilty man and a holy God. His work of intercession on behalf of the world has been Daily.

The Sin Offering

From time to time, offerings were made by individuals for specific sins. This sacrifice was conducted on the Altar of Burnt offering and was ultimately consumed by fire. Here the sinner placed his hands on the head of his offering and confessed his sin. With his own hand, the sinner then took the life of the sacrificial lamb. After the lamb or goat was killed, the priest deposited some blood on the horns of the Altar of Burnt offering. God's purpose was to teach Israel that sin could only be transferred from the sinner by blood. (Leviticus 6:24-30) The blood on the horns provided evidence that the sin had been transferred. Again, this ritual from ancient times is a crude model of what Jesus has been doing in Heaven since Adam and Eve presented their first sin offering. Jesus receives our prayers confessing our sins. He then adds to our petition His blood which was shed for our sins and He presents the sins before the Father and forgiveness is granted.

An important contrast

The difference between the daily offering and the sin offering is significant. The Daily was a corporate offering on behalf of the nation of Israel, while the sin offering was a specific offering for personal sin.

The sins of Israel were transferred into the sanctuary by these two offerings throughout the year. The corporate offering (the Daily) provided corporate atonement; the personal offering (the sin offering) was a personal service seeking atonement. At the end of each religious year, on the 10th day of the seventh month, the horns of both altars were cleansed and the record of sin was forever removed.

The Day of Atonement

On the 10th day of the seventh month, Israel faced a yearly judgment day known as the Day of Atonement. The word "atonement" simply means reconciliation, a bringing together or at-one-ment. This day always fell on the 10th day of the seventh month and this day was a special Sabbath day, for no work was done on this day regardless of the day of the week it fell on. (Leviticus 16:29) The people of Israel were required to stand before God in person on this day to account for their deeds during the past year. Only the high priest officiated in the temple services on the Day of Atonement.

Other priests that normally served in the temple throughout the year could not represent Israel before God on this day. The high priest had to go through an interesting process before he could represent the nation of Israel in the most holy compartment of the sanctuary. *He had to be found worthy of conducting this work before he could officiate on behalf of Israel!* (Leviticus 16:13)

The high priest had to *personally* provide a great sacrifice and present the blood of his sacrifice in the most holy portion of the sanctuary on the Day of Atonement *before* he could officiate on behalf of Israel. With trembling and reverence, the high priest entered the second room of the sanctuary on this special day to stand in the Holy presence of God.

The service on this day focused on the cleansing of the sanctuary. All year long, the sins of the people had been transferred to the sanctuary through the blood of the offerings. On this special day of atonement, the sanctuary was restored to its original spotless condition by the high priest. This was symbolically done when the high priest wiped the blood off the horns of the altars. Then, he wiped his bloody hands on the head of the scape goat. Thus, the record of sins was transferred from the sanctuary to the scape goat.

These three services demonstrate the basic elements of the plan of salvation. The Daily demonstrates unmerited justification (the gift of God), the sin offering demonstrates sanctification (the response of man for oneness with God) and the Day of Atonement demonstrates the final judgment and disposition of sin (the consummation of salvation). These elements combine to explain the importance of the throwing down of the censer in Revelation 8:5.

The censer thrown down

Revelation 8:2-5 says nothing about *why* the censer is thrown down. John just says that the angel ministering at the Altar of Incense places a lot of incense on the altar. Then he throws down the censer which is followed by an earthquake and other physical manifestations on earth.

The setting gives us two clues about the meaning of this event. First, the Altar of Incense is the altar for the services of the Daily. Second, the censer is a device used during the atonement process. (See Numbers 16.) The throwing down of the censer indicates that the atonement process going on at the Altar of Incense is finished. The censer is no longer necessary. Revelation 8:2-5 also suggests that some of God's children are waiting expectantly for the censer to be thrown down, for this is why their prayers ascend before God's throne. They anticipate the events that follow and when the physical manifestations occur on earth (earthquake, lightning, etc.), they know what has taken place in Heaven!

The throwing down of the censer occurs because earth's cup of iniquity is filled. Time has run out. Sin reaches its full measure when we finish the 70th Jubilee! Notice these timing patterns from the past:

- In Noah's day, the antediluvians filled up their cup when the 120 years of mercy expired. (Genesis 6:3)

- In Moses' day, the Amorites filled up their cup at the time of the Exodus. (Genesis 15:16)

- Israel was sent into Babylonian captivity when they violated 70 Sabbatical years. (2 Chronicles 36:21)

- Israel lost their opportunity as trustees of the gospel when they violated the 70 weeks. (Matthew 21:43)

- The time allotted to Israel turns out to be exactly 30 Jubilees.

- The Christian Church's opportunity expired at the completion of 36 Jubilees of time (1798). (Daniel 7:25)

The Daily ends

The corporate intercession of Christ on behalf of the world ends when the censer is thrown down. God's judgments, the seven trumpets, will follow. During the time period of the trumpets, the gospel will go to every person and each person will make a decision — for or against the gospel. As each person makes his choice, God seals him in his decision. Every person will either worship God as He commands or they will eventually acquiesce and obey the devil for the sake of survival. The point here is that all human beings are going to face a time when they will either obey God or Satan. There will be no middle ground. When every person has made his choice, the seventh trumpet will sound and salvation's offer will be withdrawn from the world.

My point is that the throwing down of the censer marks the end of corporate intercession on behalf of the world as a unit. On the other hand, the seventh trumpet of Revelation marks the end of mercy for individuals. In ancient times, the Feast of Trumpets began on the first day of the seventh month (our September or October). For this reason, I suspect the casting down of the censer and the confirming earthquake could happen in the fall of 1994. However, there is one factor that could temporarily delay the earthquake and the commencement of the Great Tribulation. It is the selection of the 144,000. (Revelation 7:1-4)

The sanctuary service holds the key to understanding the prophetic pieces of Daniel and Revelation. First, when the *daily* ministry of Christ is removed, a sin-full world is exposed to the wrath of a holy God. During the time period of the trumpets, Jesus offers Himself to individuals as the only acceptable sin offering the Father will receive. Those who accept Christ and the terms of His salvation will receive full pardon because this will be the great time of judgment, the time when every human being alive will be judged by the Creator of Heaven and Earth. Just as the Day of Atonement in ancient Israel came on time each year (tenth day of the seventh month), so will the coming actions of God occur on time. I believe 70 Jubilee cycles (or 490 weeks of years) mark the limits of God's patience and the time for God's visitation has come.

Note: Remember, God punished Israel when they reached 70 Sabbatical violations and at the end of 70 "sevens." It also appears that God will destroy sin at the end of 70 centuries (7,000 years), too. Will God begin the judgment of man soon after the conclusion of 70 Jubilees? I believe so.

Daniel 12:11,12 explains a mystery. Notice, **"From the time that the daily sacrifice is abolished and the abomination that causes desolation is set up, there will be 1,290 days. Blessed is the one who waits for and reaches the end of the 1,335 days."** (Daniel 12:12) From the time the Daily (the services of Jesus in Heaven) is abolished until the universal death decree on God's children is enacted (the abomination that causes desolation), there will be 1,290 literal days. But, those who can endure until the end of the 1,335 days will be especially blessed, for they shall see Jesus in all His glory with their own eyes! What makes this text so fascinating is this: If you add 1,335 days to the fall of 1994, you easily reach a year that appears to be the 6,000th year since sin — 1998. In other words, 1,335 days may be the actual number of days required to synchronize the Jubilee cycles with the seventh millennium.

Bible Theme #4 — Revelation's time periods and 1994

There is a prophetic mechanism that says: *Prophetic things are only understood on or about the time of fulfillment.* The understanding of Revelation is now open for study and investigation because the things described there are about to be fulfilled. God has kept these things hidden until now so that our discovery of His truth would motivate us to prepare for His appearing.

There are many time periods mentioned in Revelation. For example, there will be 42 months of persecution by Babylon. (Revelation 13:5) The 144,000 will be empowered by the Two Witnesses for 1,260 days. (Revelation 11:3) The torment of the fifth trumpet will last five literal months. (Revelation 9:5) The millennium is 1,000 literal years in length. The point here is these time periods carefully harmonize with the operation of the Jubilee calendar. These time periods are literal units of time because the Jubilee calendar with its day/year mechanism has expired.

God is giving good clues about the meaning of Revelation. Scientists are predicting the same things predicted in Revelation. In fact, they are doing the work of ministers who are unwilling to investigate the book of Revelation, and consequently, are failing to warn the world of God's wrath! World conditions are ripe for a catastrophic conclusion. There is much talk of peace and safety, but the hearts of many have waxed cold. There is no love, peace, or safety outside of Jesus. As in Noah's day, the world is beyond restoration. Politicians can only offer an illusion that we can solve the complex problems that face us.

Present truth

Truth is like a bulb that lies hidden in the soil. At the proper time each Spring, the bulb begins to grow. Once the flower of *present truth* opens, its beauty cannot be silenced. Hope and encouragement radiate from beauty. In a similar way, these four great Bible themes have come together to help us understand that we are living in the last days.

It has not been possible in this brief appendix to prove every point. In fact, I may not be able to prove many points to your satisfaction. In the final analysis though, I have tried to bring hope. The coming of Jesus is imminent. The Holy Spirit bears witness of this fact. So, let's get ready to go home by seeking purity of heart and character. Let's do everything we can to invite our loved ones and friends and even those we do not know to come along. What do you say to that?

Summary

Four Bible themes indicate that Jubilee year 1994 could be an ominous year. The first theme points to the seventh millennium. We see that the crown-jewel of the weekly cycle serves as a template of the coming "Sabbatical Millennium." I pointed out that the seventh millennium has to begin on time, for God's purposes know no haste nor delay. Those who live during the Great Tribulation will see just how important God's holy day is to our Creator. Just as the Sabbath year was a test of faith to Israel of old, the Sabbath *day*, the seventh day of the week, shall be a "Sabbath-rest test" to the remnant of Israel.

The second theme shows that the weekly cycle serves as a template of the Jubilee cycle. We learned that God's patience with Israel was reached with 70 violations of Sabbatical years, then He removed them as trustees of the gospel after they had filled up 70 weeks of violation. The Jubilee cycles point out that God's patience with man has a limit. Just as the Jubilee cycles began with the 1437 B.C. Exodus, the Jubilee cycles ended on March 19, 1994. Soon, the 144,000 will receive great Holy Spirit power and they will present the truth about God that will be so present and so essential for our time. Billions will hear their message and millions will be saved as a result.

The third theme chronologically assembles the timing of the major pieces. Specifically, Jesus could end His corporate mediatorial work (the Daily) in 1994 and the final phase of the great judgment of man could begin. If this happens to be the case, the 1,335 days of Daniel 12 could commence which would carry us down to or near the 6,000th year! Do the 1,335 days serve to synchronize the conclusion of 70 Jubilees with the arrival of the 6,000th year? Perhaps. Even if the Great Tribulation is delayed beyond 1994, the Sabbatical millennium will still begin on time. We are speeding toward a rendezvous with the Almighty. Apocalyptic prophecy does not provide detail sufficient for pinpointing *any* future date, but it does provide sufficient detail for those who want to know what God's plans are.

The fourth theme unfolds the intimate relationship between the time periods mentioned in Revelation and the 1,335 days of Daniel 12. Soon, the daily ministry of Jesus in Heaven will end and the seven trumpets will sound. The predicted events will take place, and the predicted time periods will serve a valuable function. People will know that there is an end to the Great Tribulation and they will know its approximate location. There is a purpose to all that God does. God has set the limits. The value of understanding Revelation's story is that God will have a people on earth who understand what He is about to do *before* He does it. God will have a people on earth who have done their homework and put their prophetic faith in order. God will have a people who are willing to go, to be and to do all that He asks. God will have a prepared people. These will go forward in the spirit and power of Elijah during the Great Tribulation and they will be especially blessed for their faith. For all of these reasons, Jubilee year 1994 and beyond appears to be ominous!

Supplemental Bible Study Helps

Bible Study Helps - Audio and Video Tapes

The following is a sample listing of seminar studies on Revelation. Tapes may be purchased individually or as a set from a seminar series, such as seen on TV. Keep in mind that each tape is a building block therefore, no one presentation is complete within itself.

1. The wrath of God and the full cup principle
2. The purpose and process of Bible prophecy
3. Who is Jesus? Why did He die for man?
4. Michael and Lucifer, the origin of sin
5. The plan of salvation
6. The timely prophecies of Daniel
7. The judgment of the living
8. Introduction to Revelation / Rules of Interpretation
9. The seven seals
10. The seven trumpets
11. The two beasts of Revelation
12. The man of sin and the 144,000
13. The two witnesses
14. The mark of the beast and God's everlasting covenant
15. The Jubilee calendar
16. The Sabbath-rest test

continued on next page

Bible Study Helps - Books and Charts

1. *The Revelation of Jesus* This book (346 pages) serves as the primary textbook for seminar study. The book not only addresses coming events, it presents a historical setting for understanding how the prophecies operate. It also contains several diagrams and charts on Daniel and Revelation.

2. **Day Star Newsletter** Our monthly newsletter usually contains Bible studies on topics that relate to current issues and/or the prophetic stories found in Daniel and Revelation. Some remaining back issues are available.

3. *18 End-Time Bible Prophecies* This book is a verse by verse commentary on the 18 apocalyptic prophecies found in Daniel and Revelation. It is written in a parallel format with the *New International Version* Bible. (282 pages)

4. *Warning! Revelation is about to be fulfilled* This book is also available in Spanish.

5. **Charts** and other study helps — call for selection and availability.

Wake Up America Seminars, Inc.

P.O. Box 273, Bellbrook, Ohio 45305

(513) 848-3322

or

P.O. Box 5003, Georgetown, Texas 78627

(512) 863-9009

Call between 9:00 am and 4:00 pm local time, Monday - Thursday for prices and availability.

Visa / Mastercard / Discover accepted.

— Proclaiming Revelation's Story —